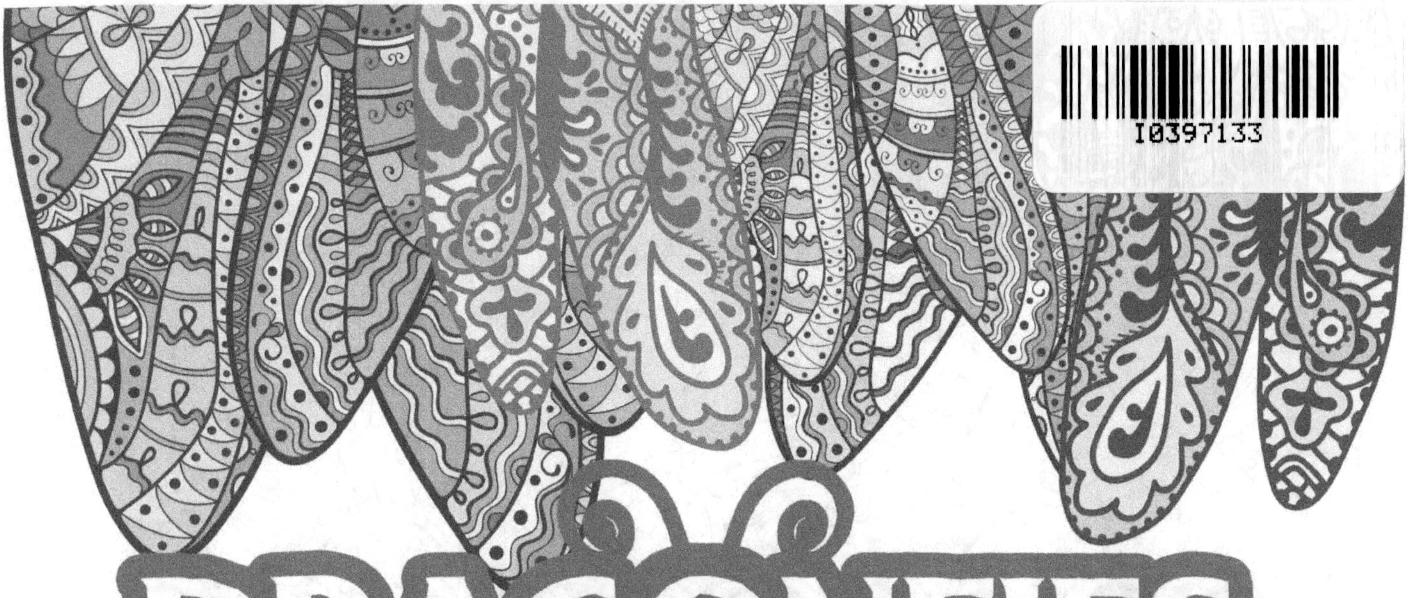

DRAGONFIES

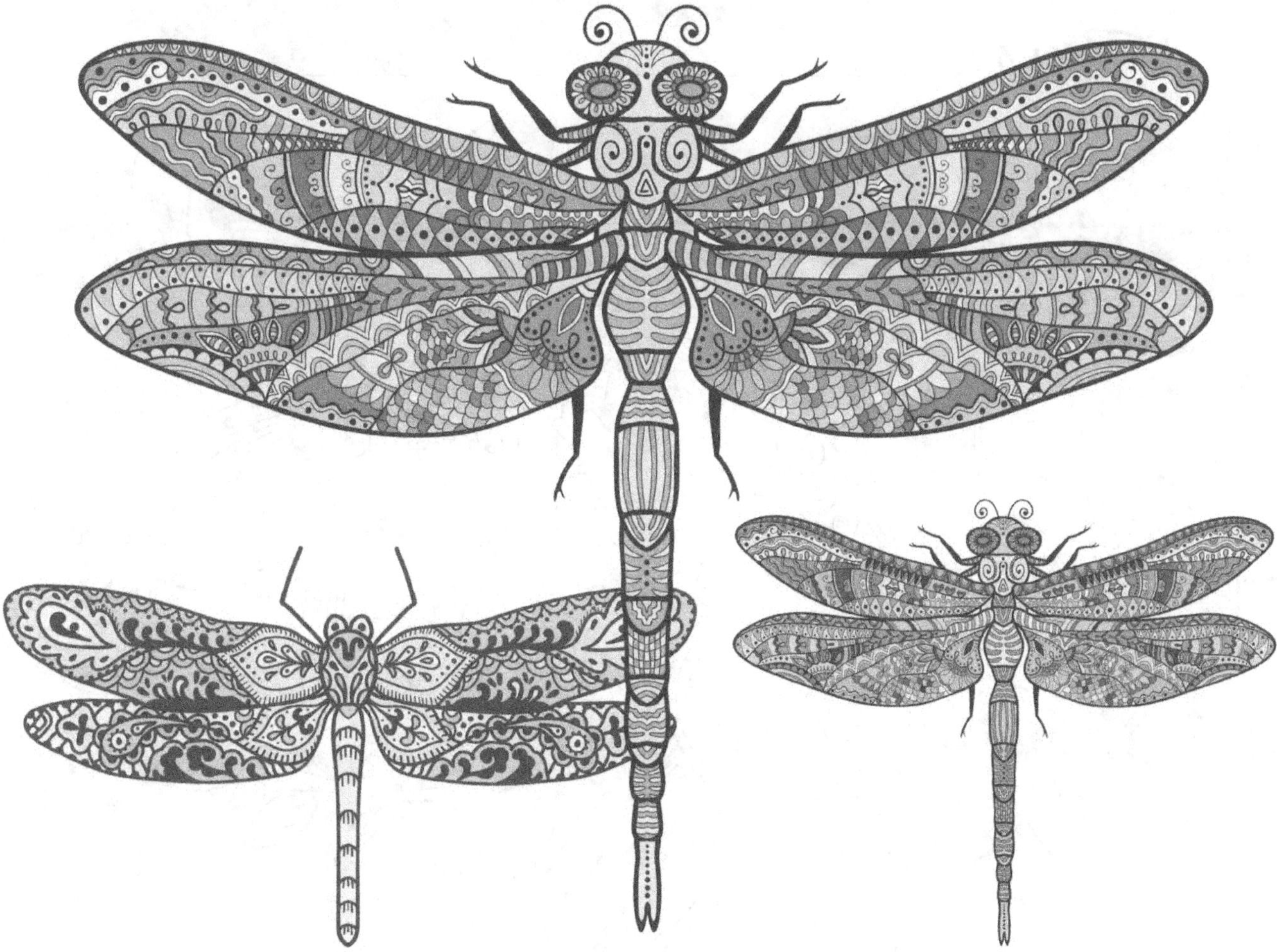

COLORING BOOK FOR ADULTS

Date : ____________________

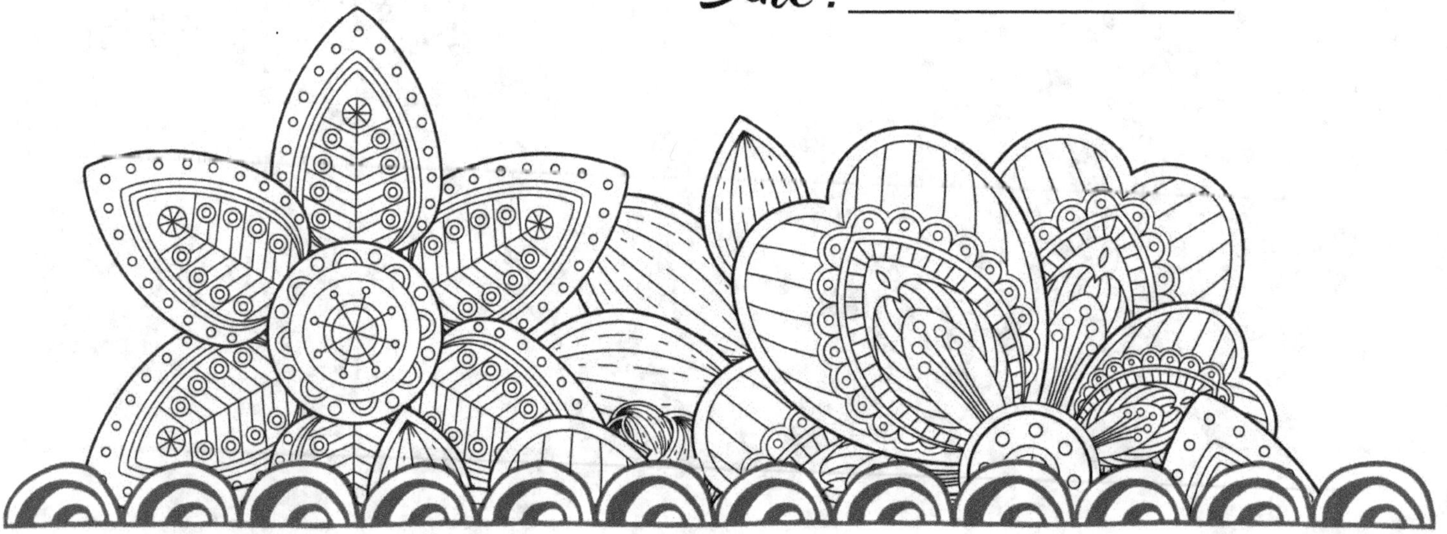

TO : ____

From : ____

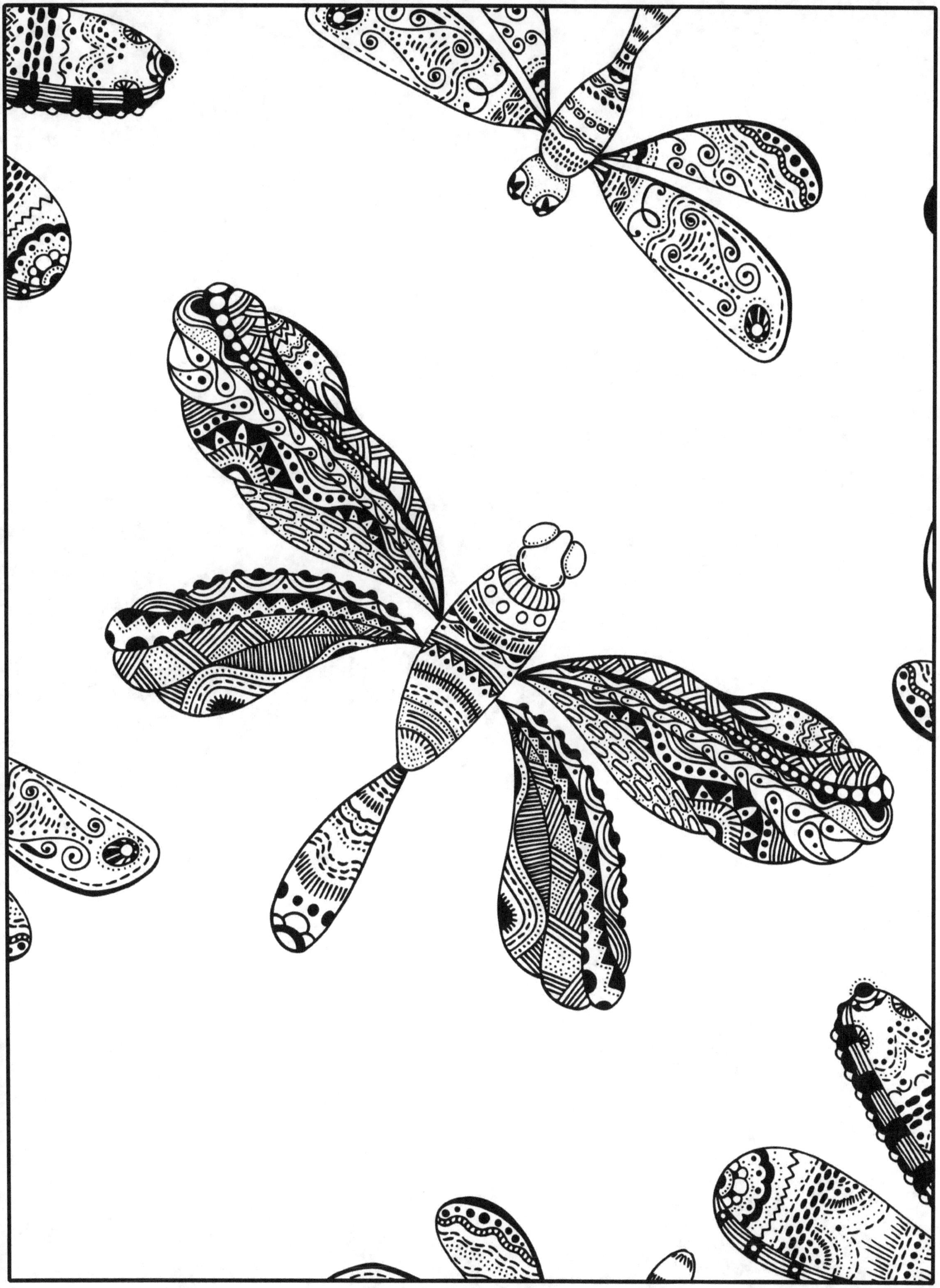

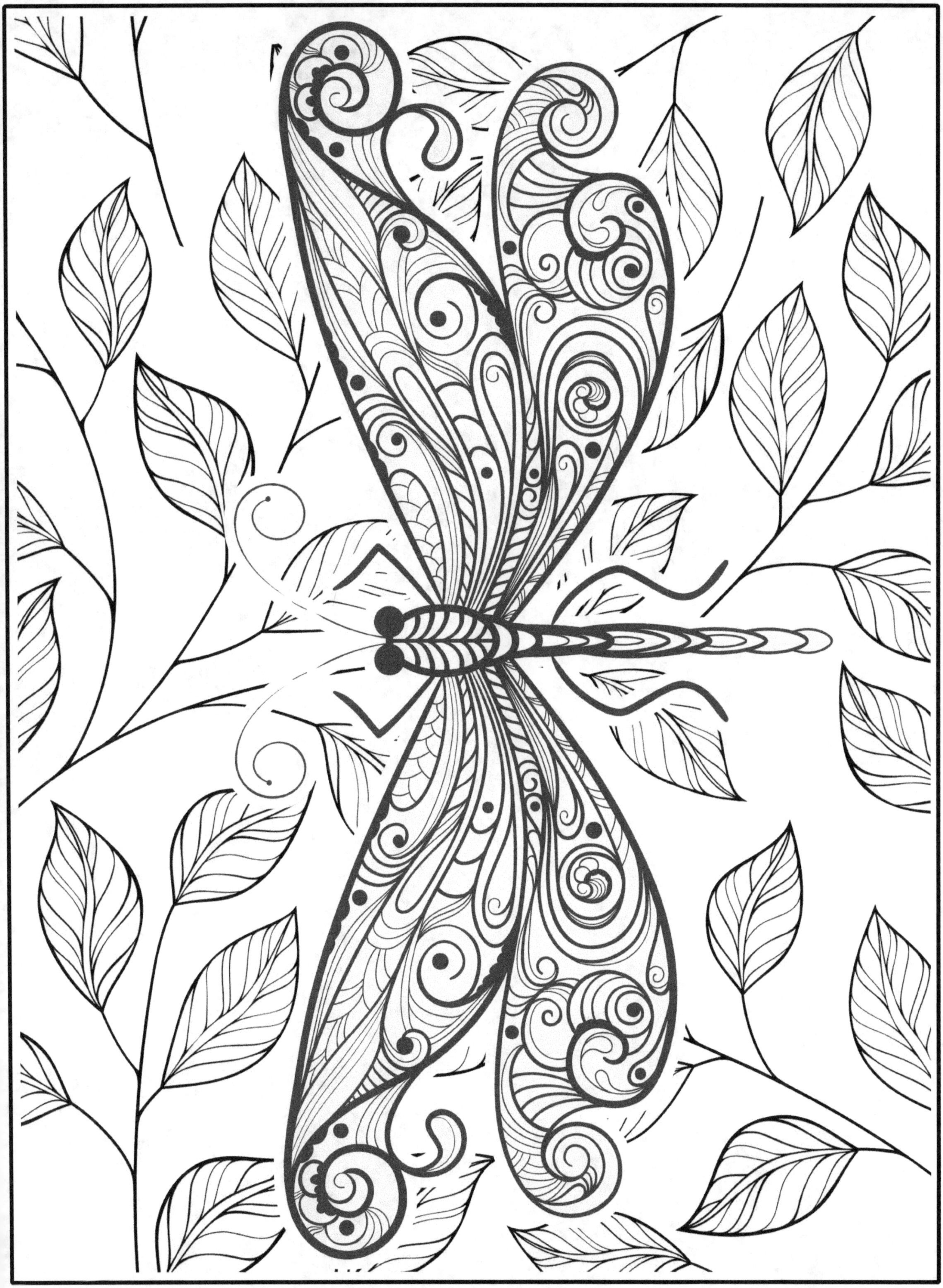

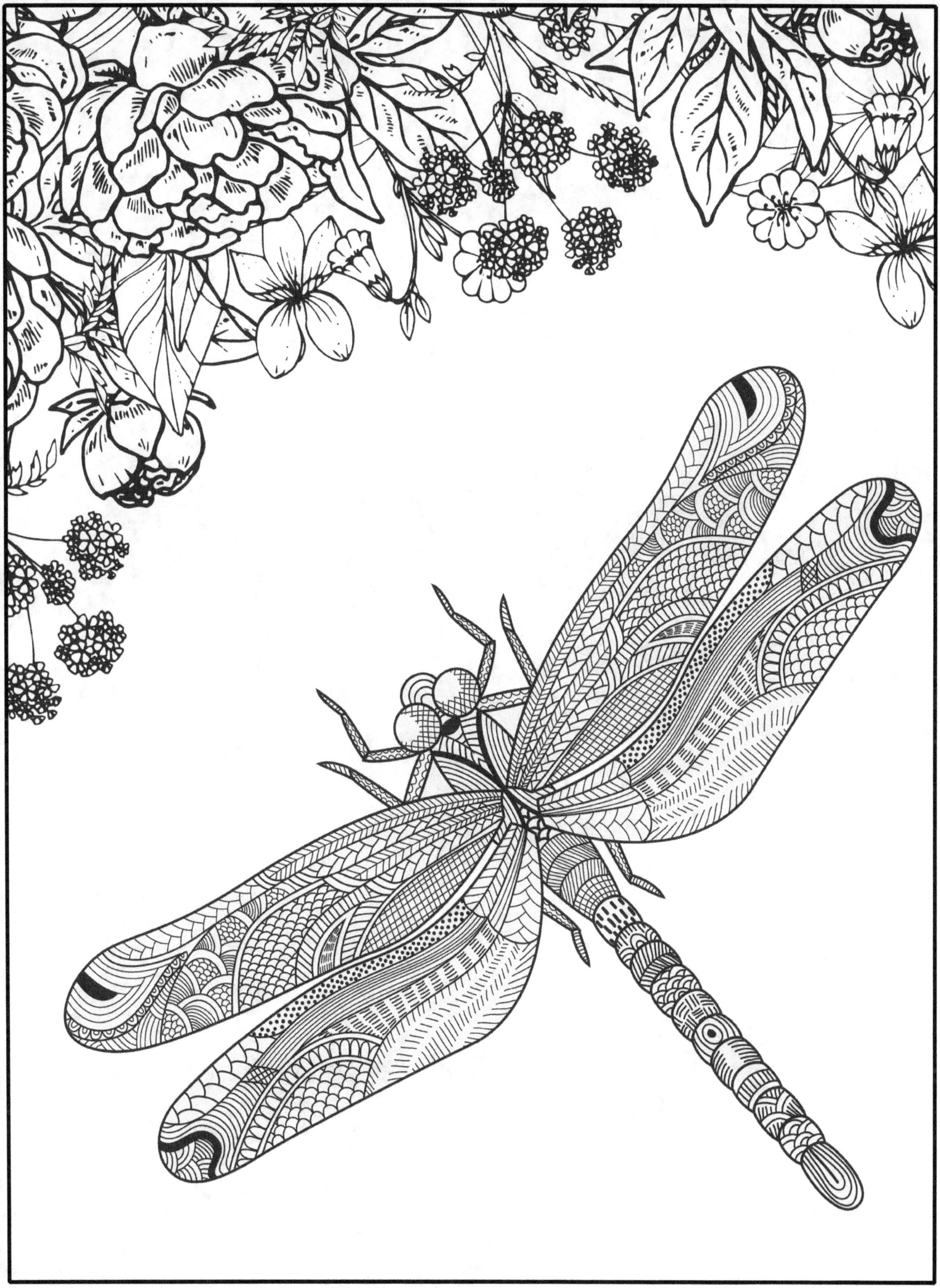

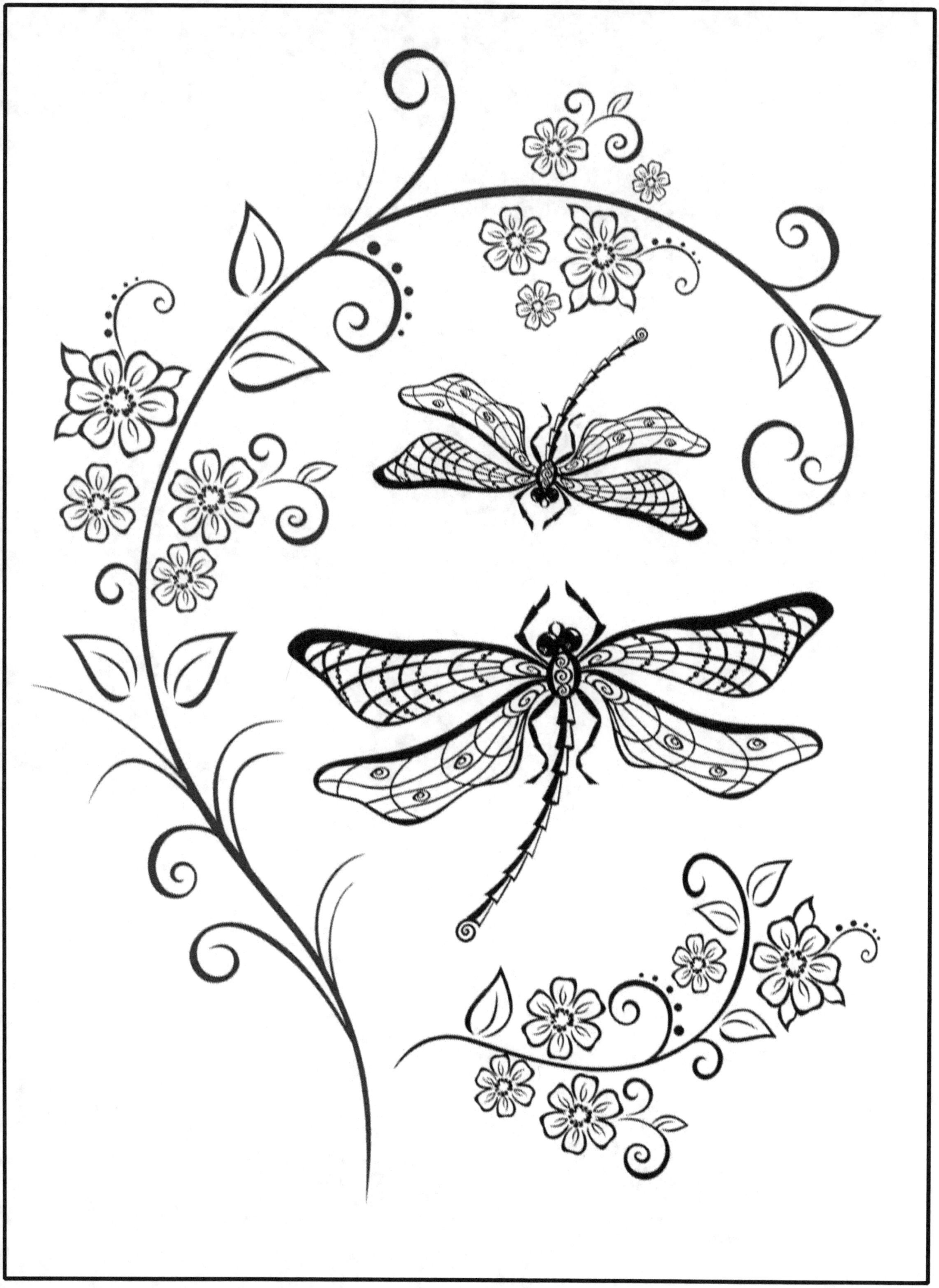

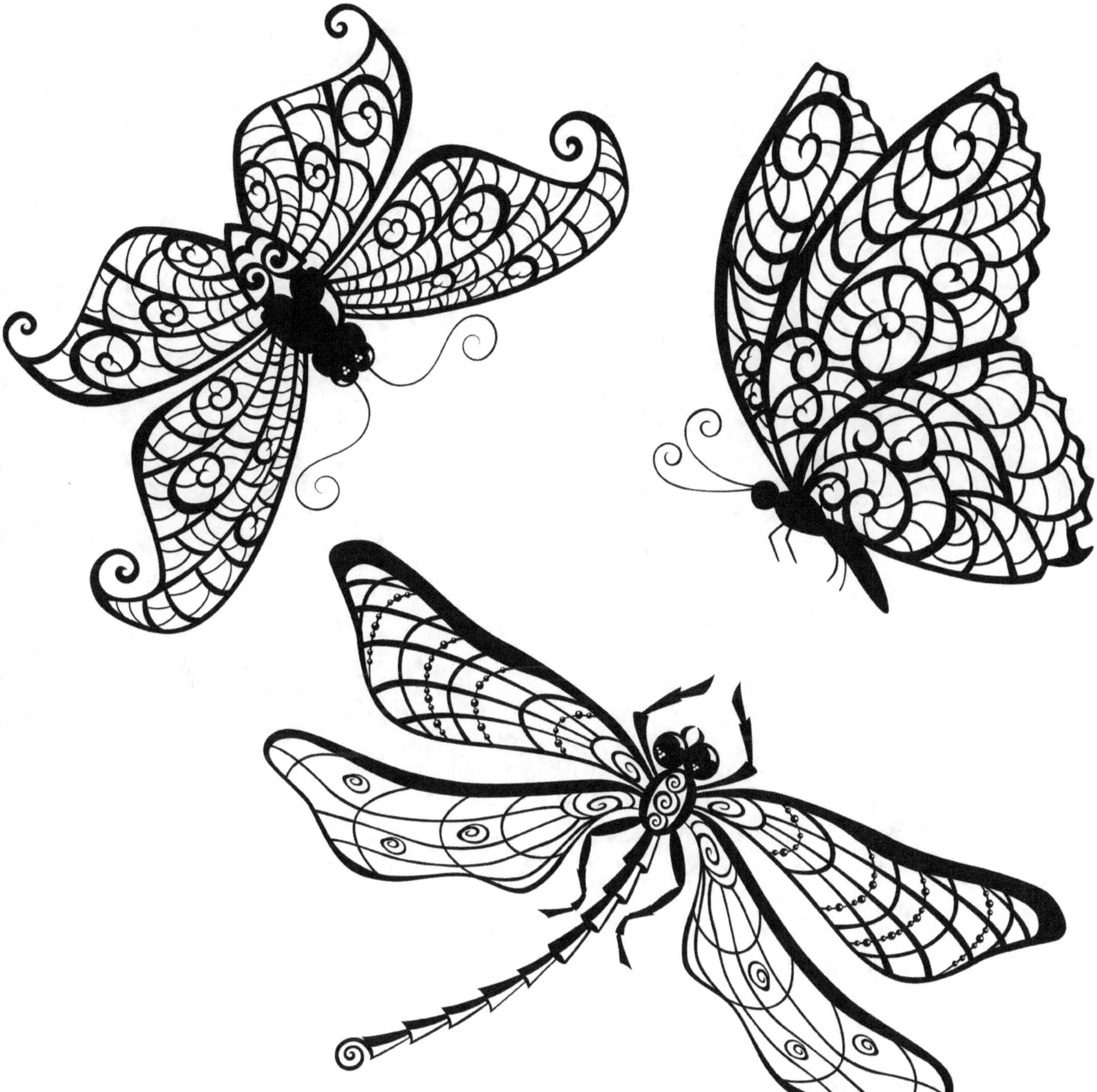

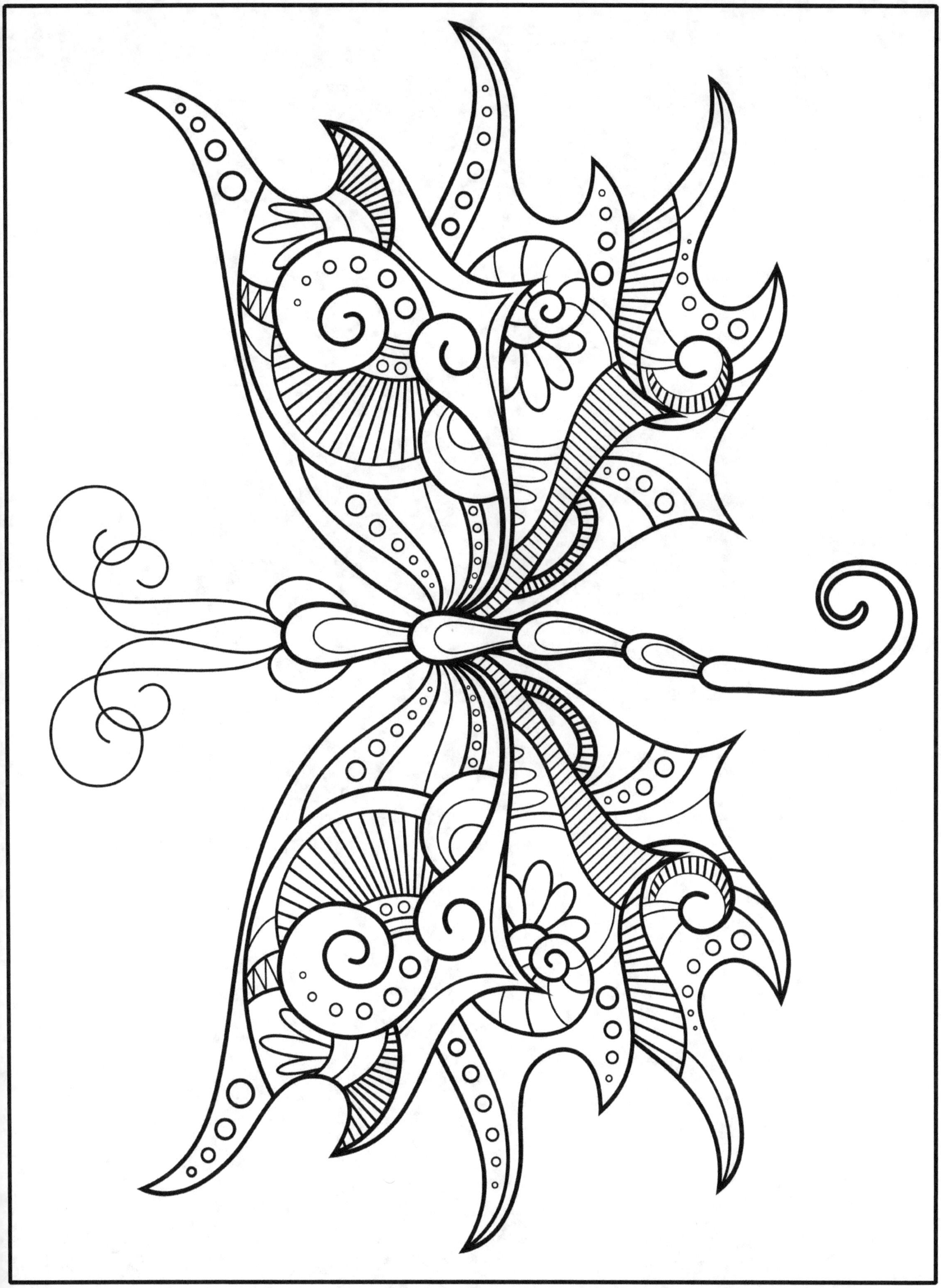

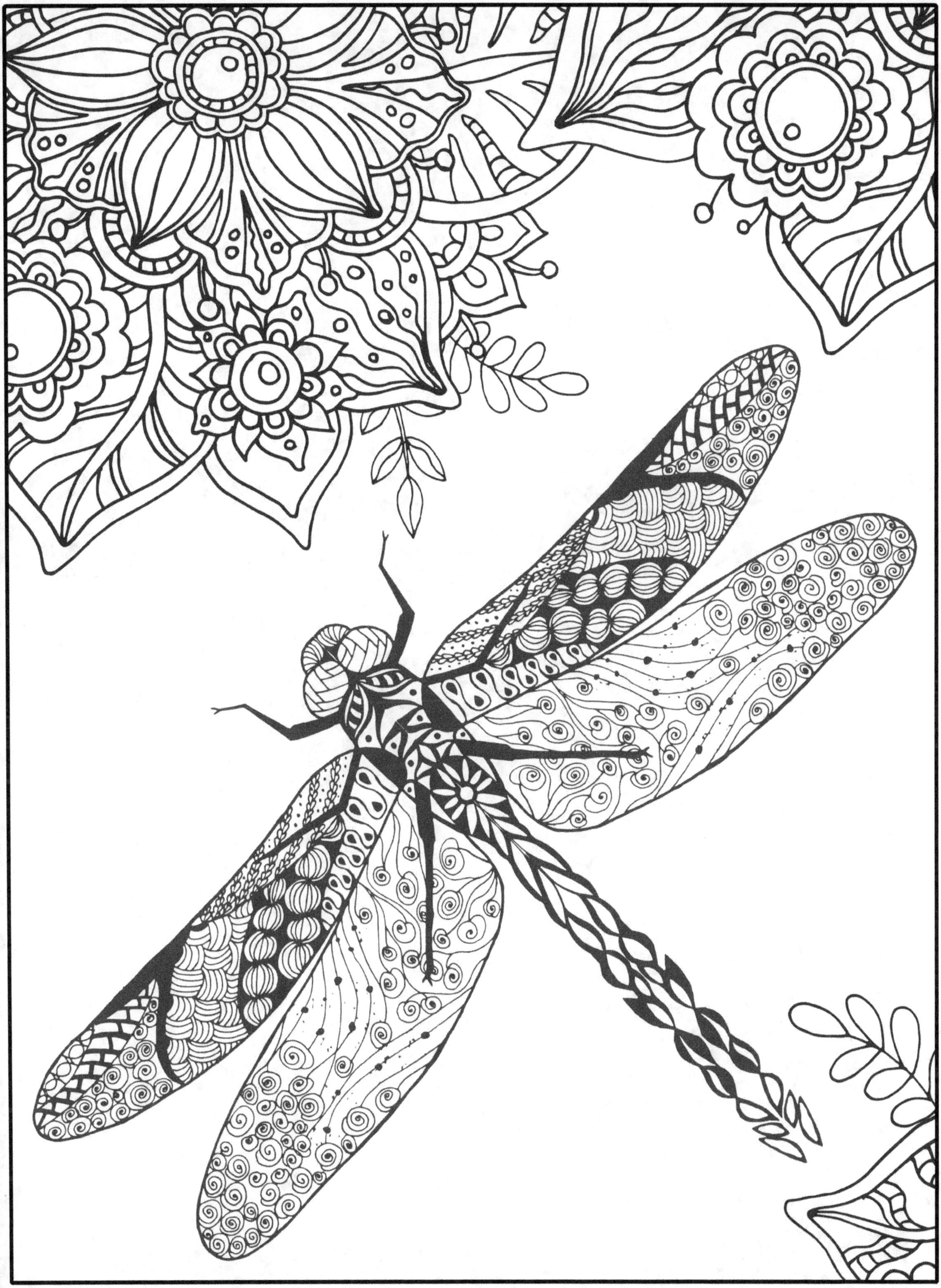

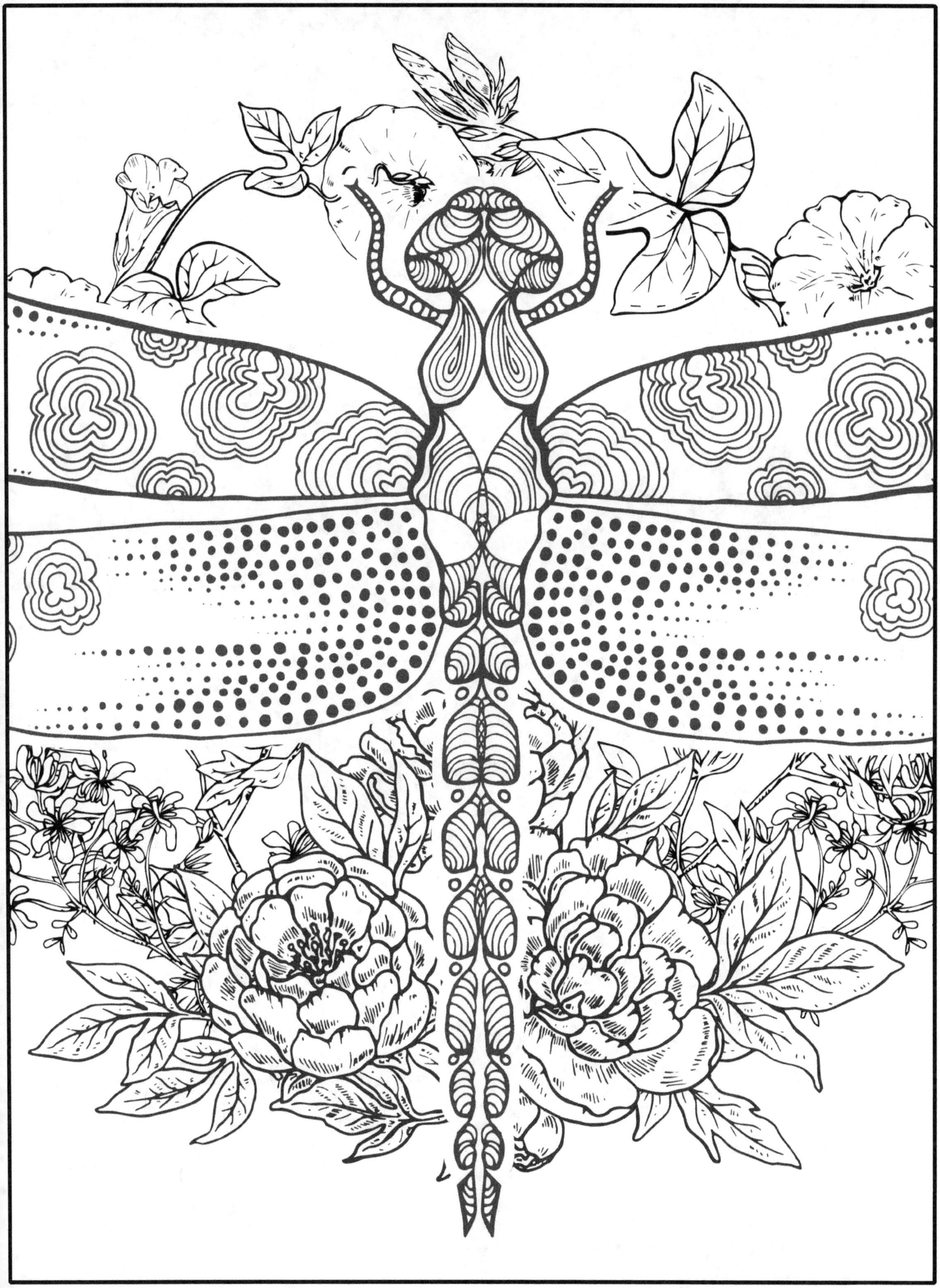

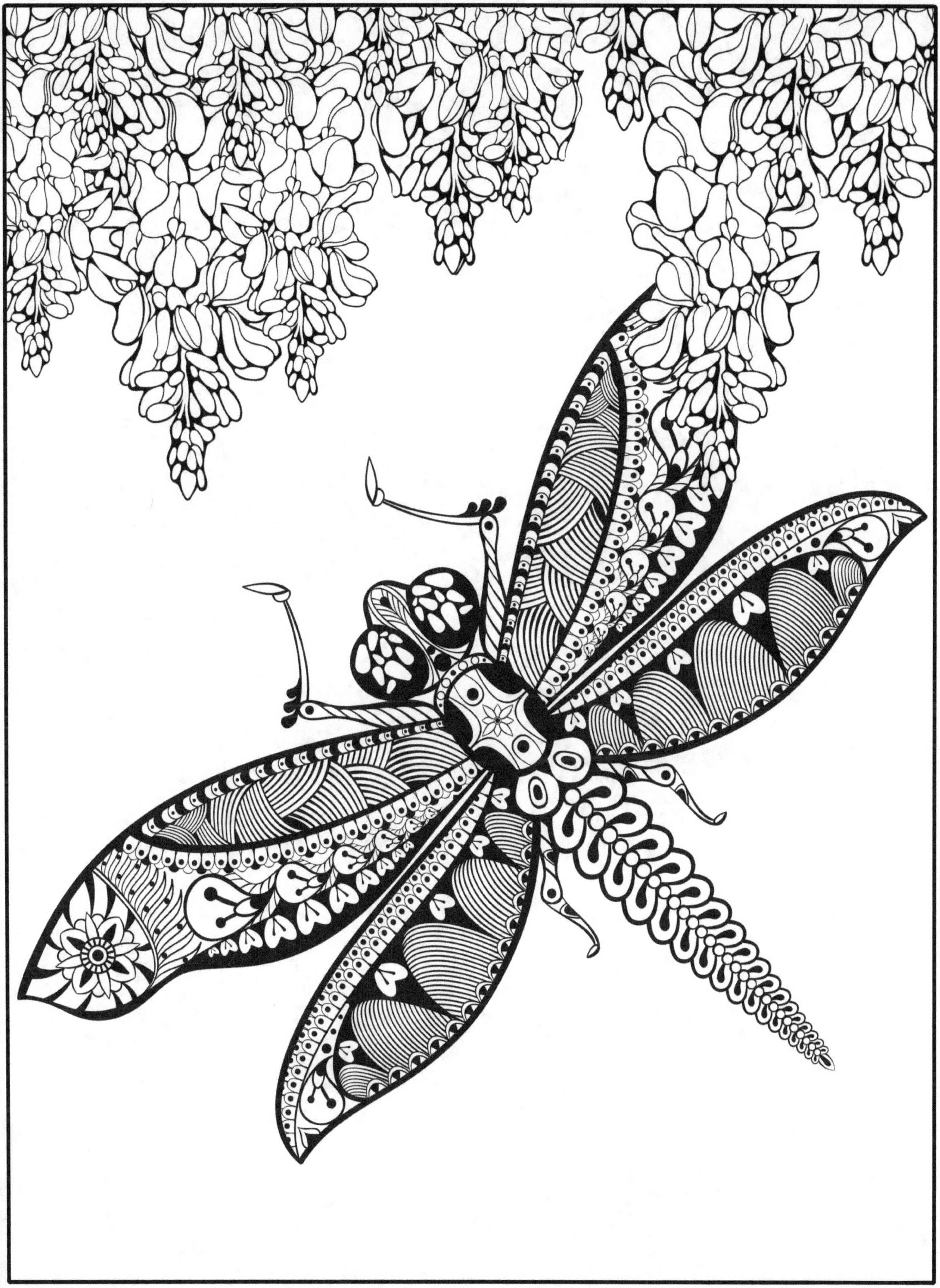

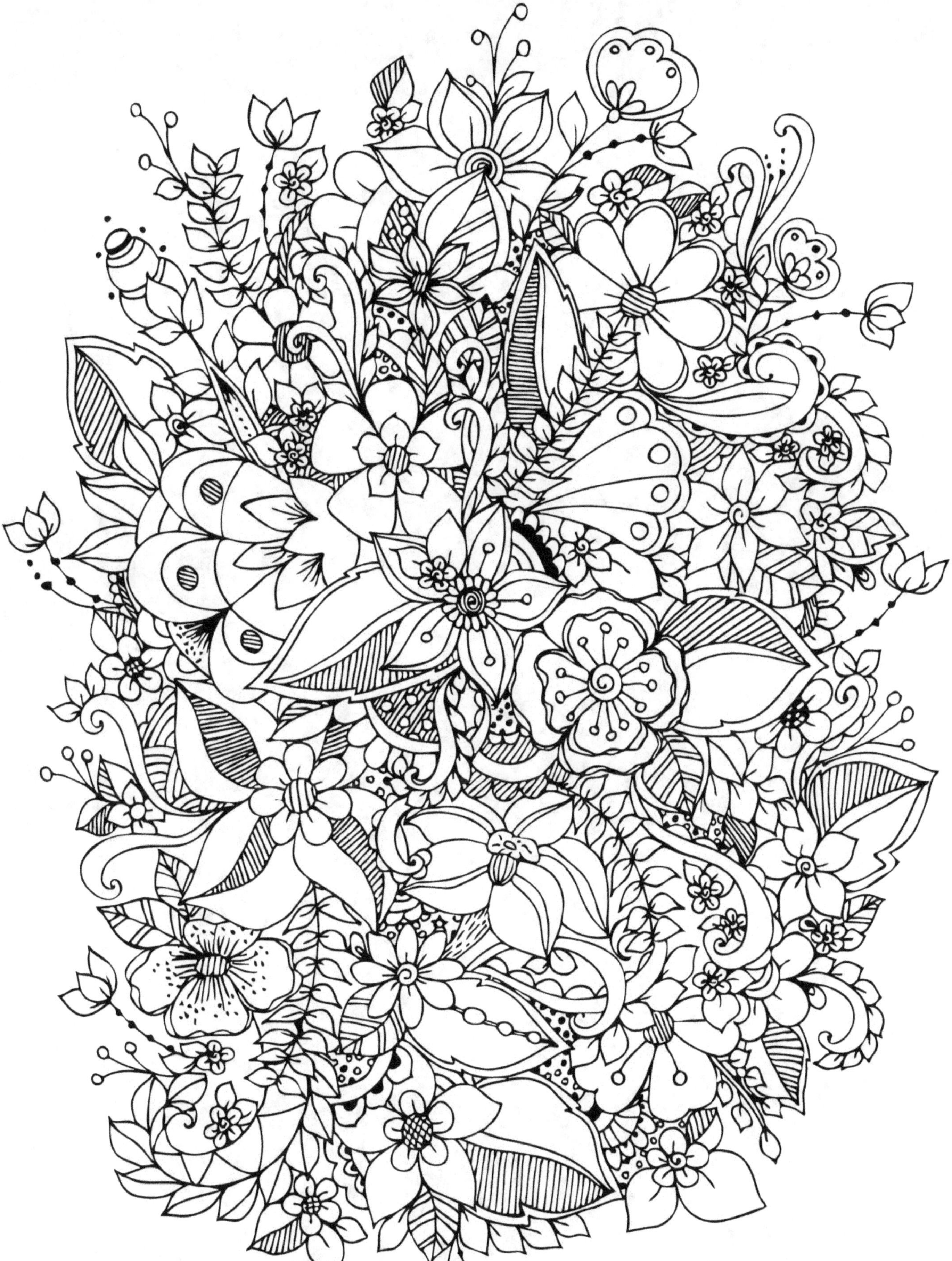

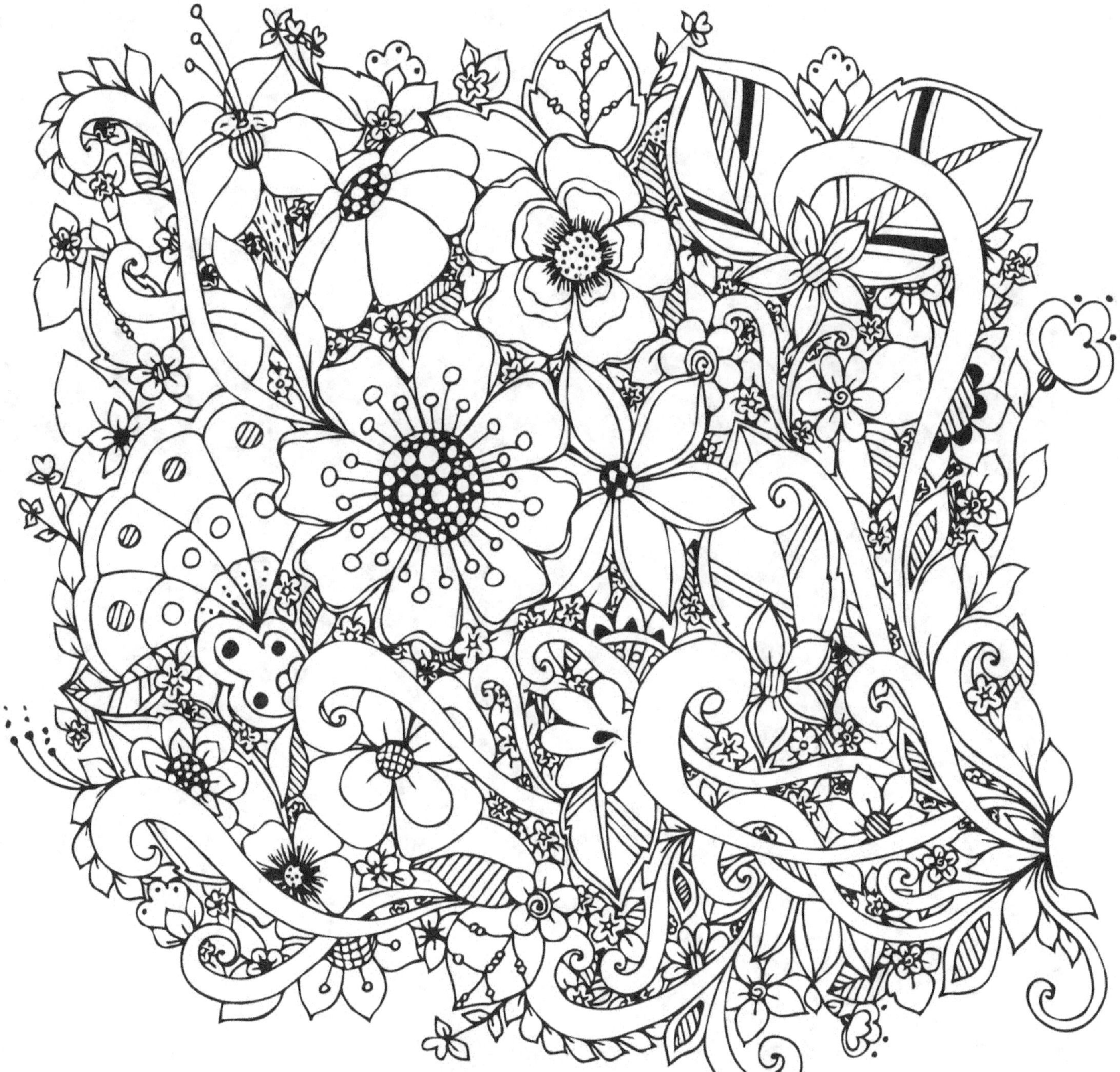

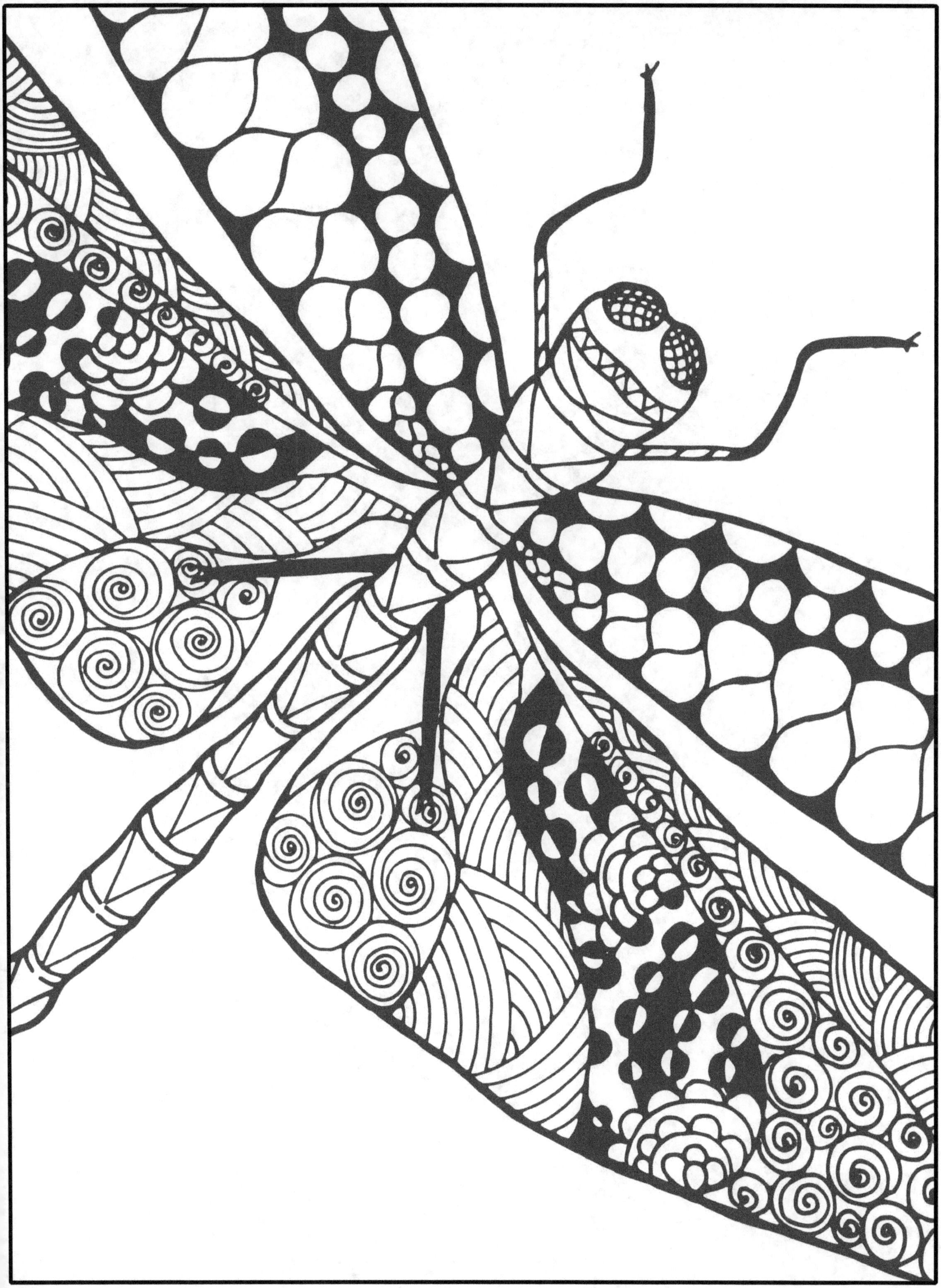

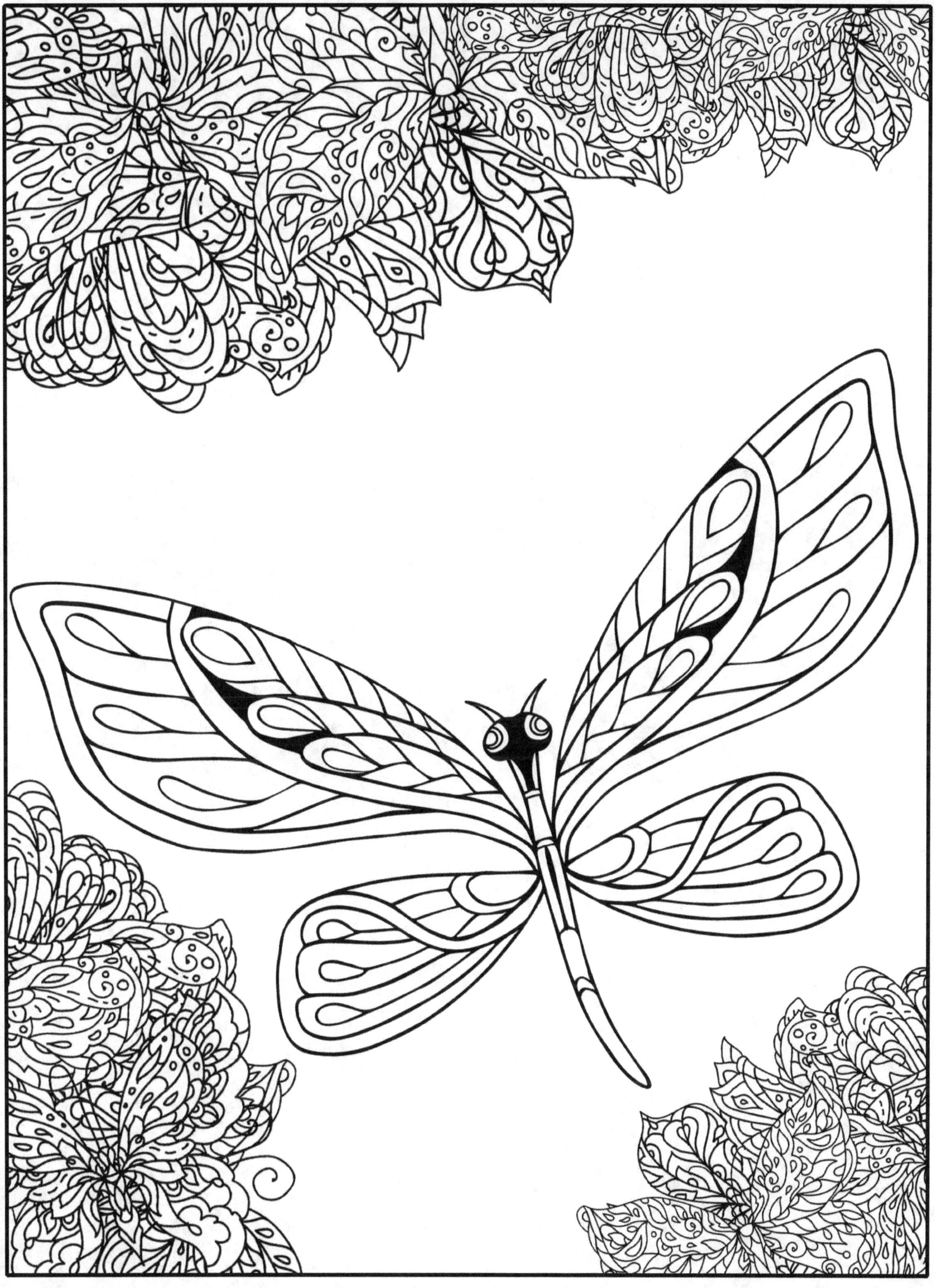

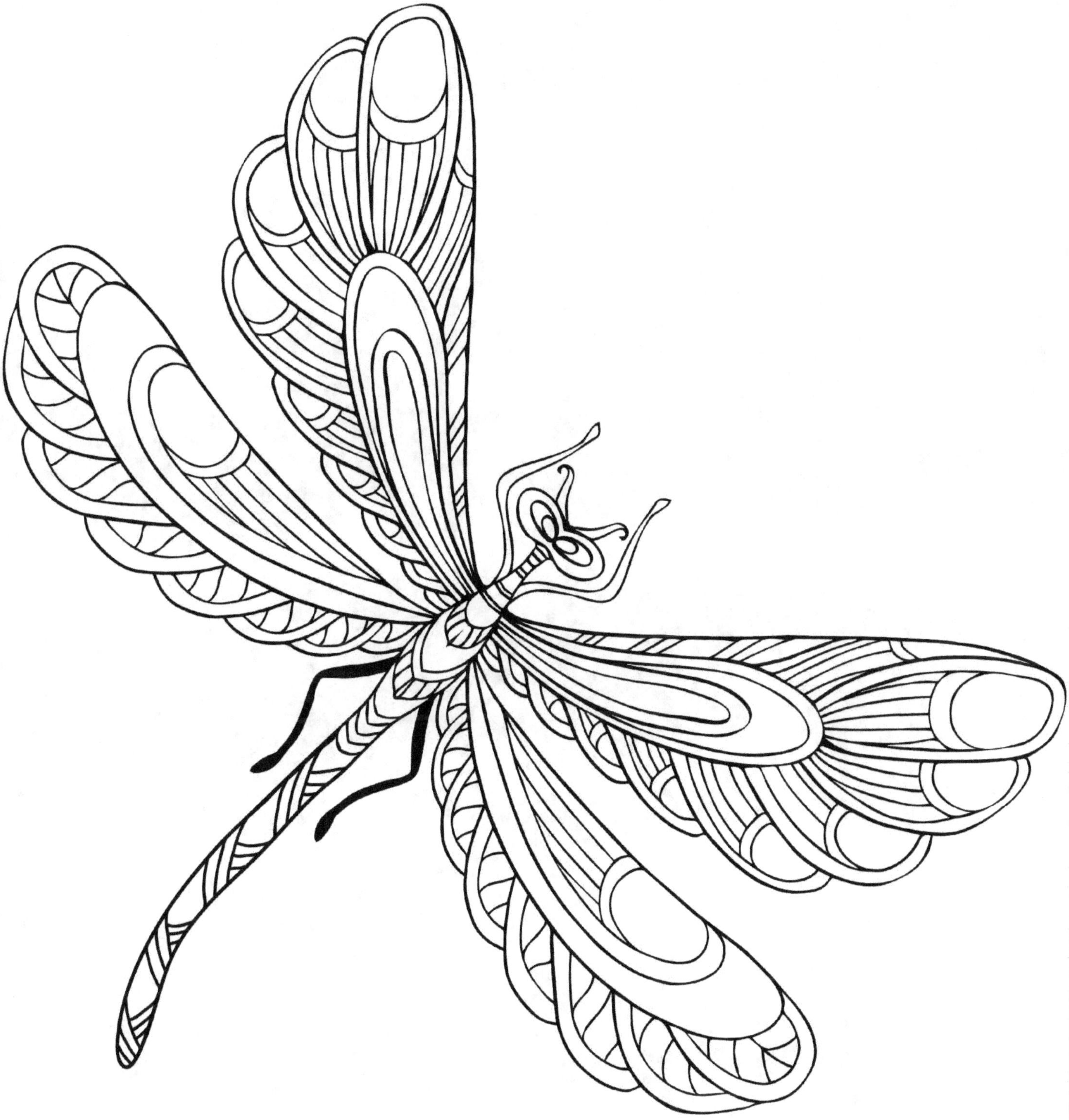

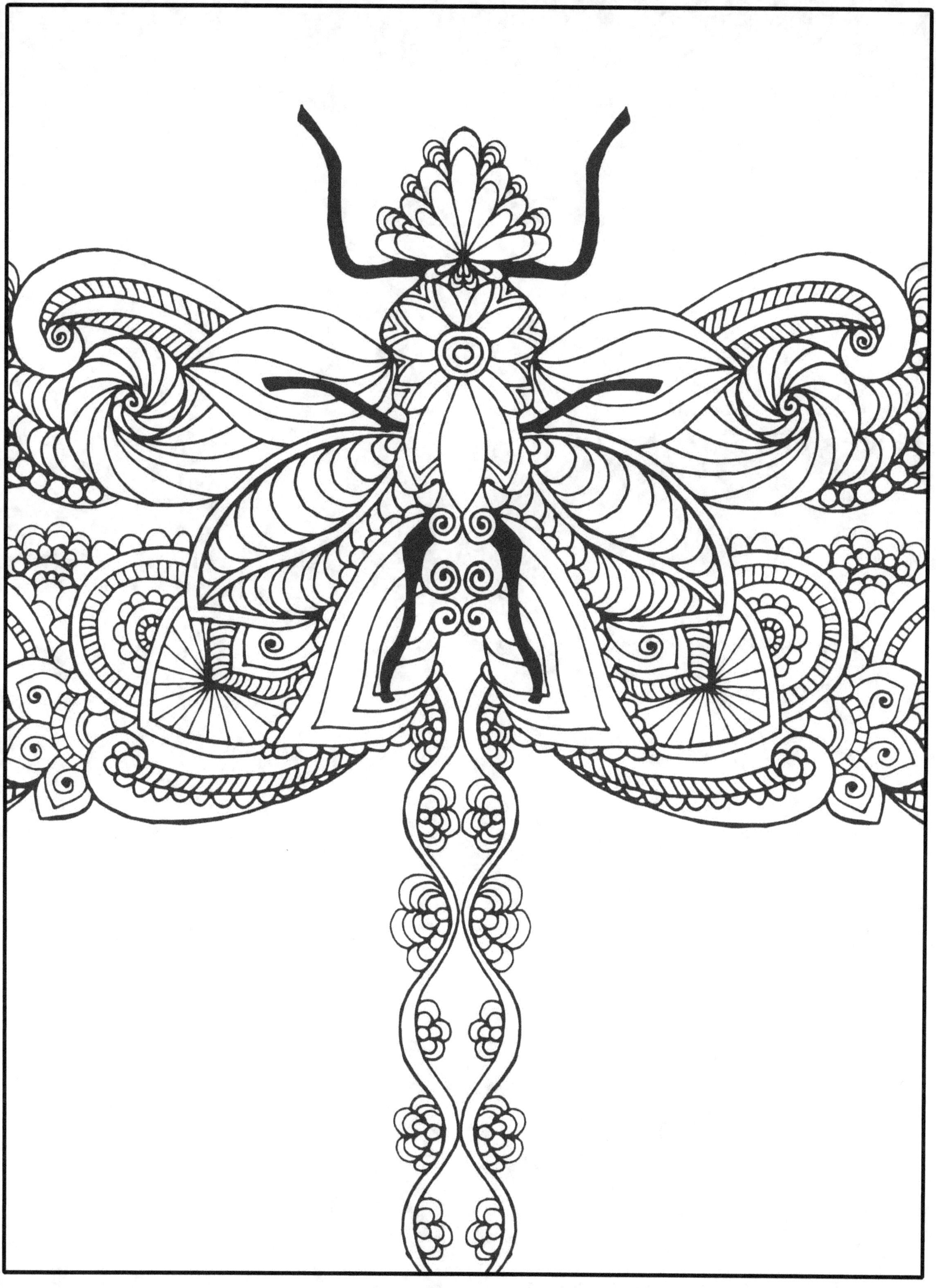

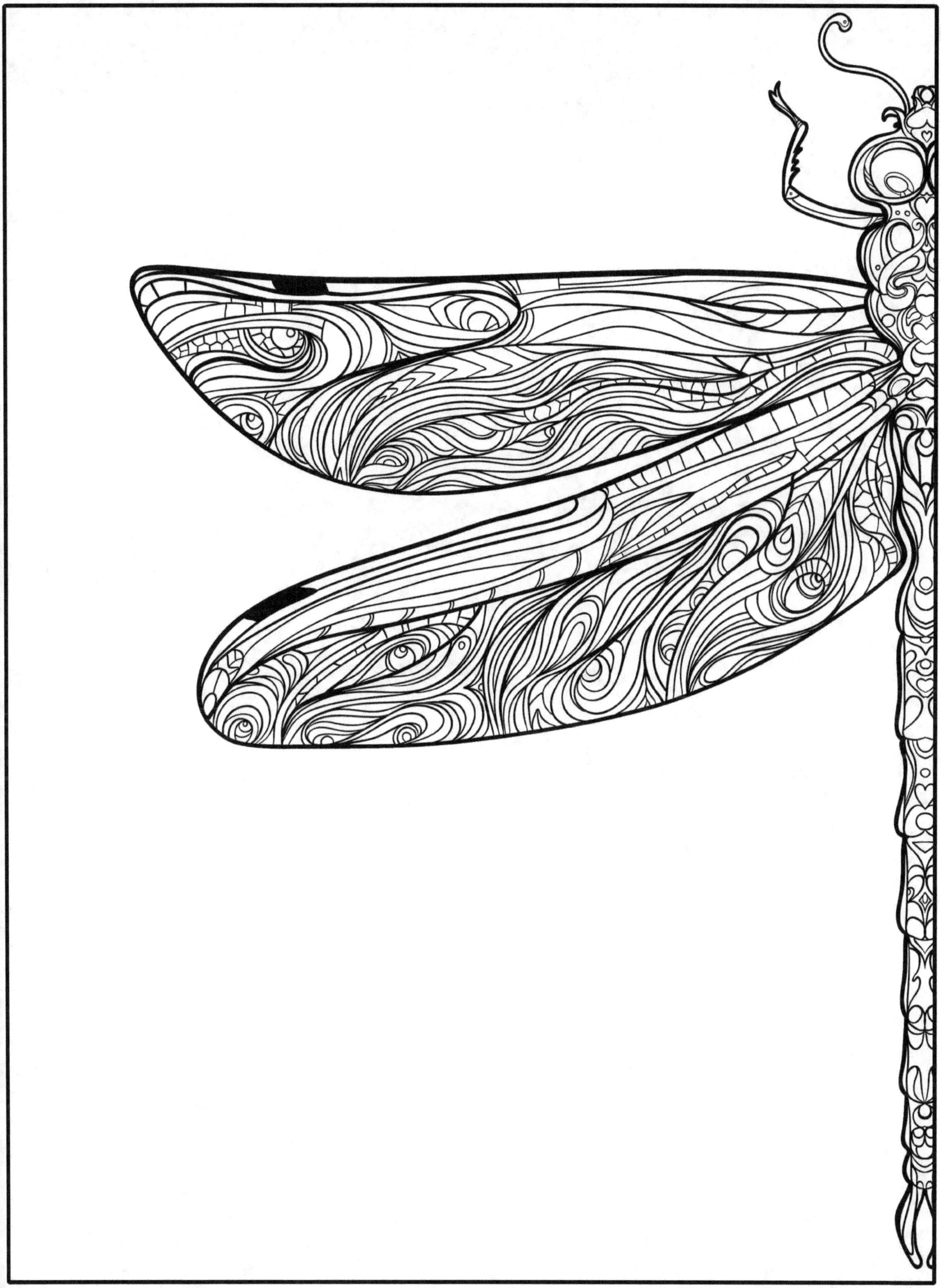

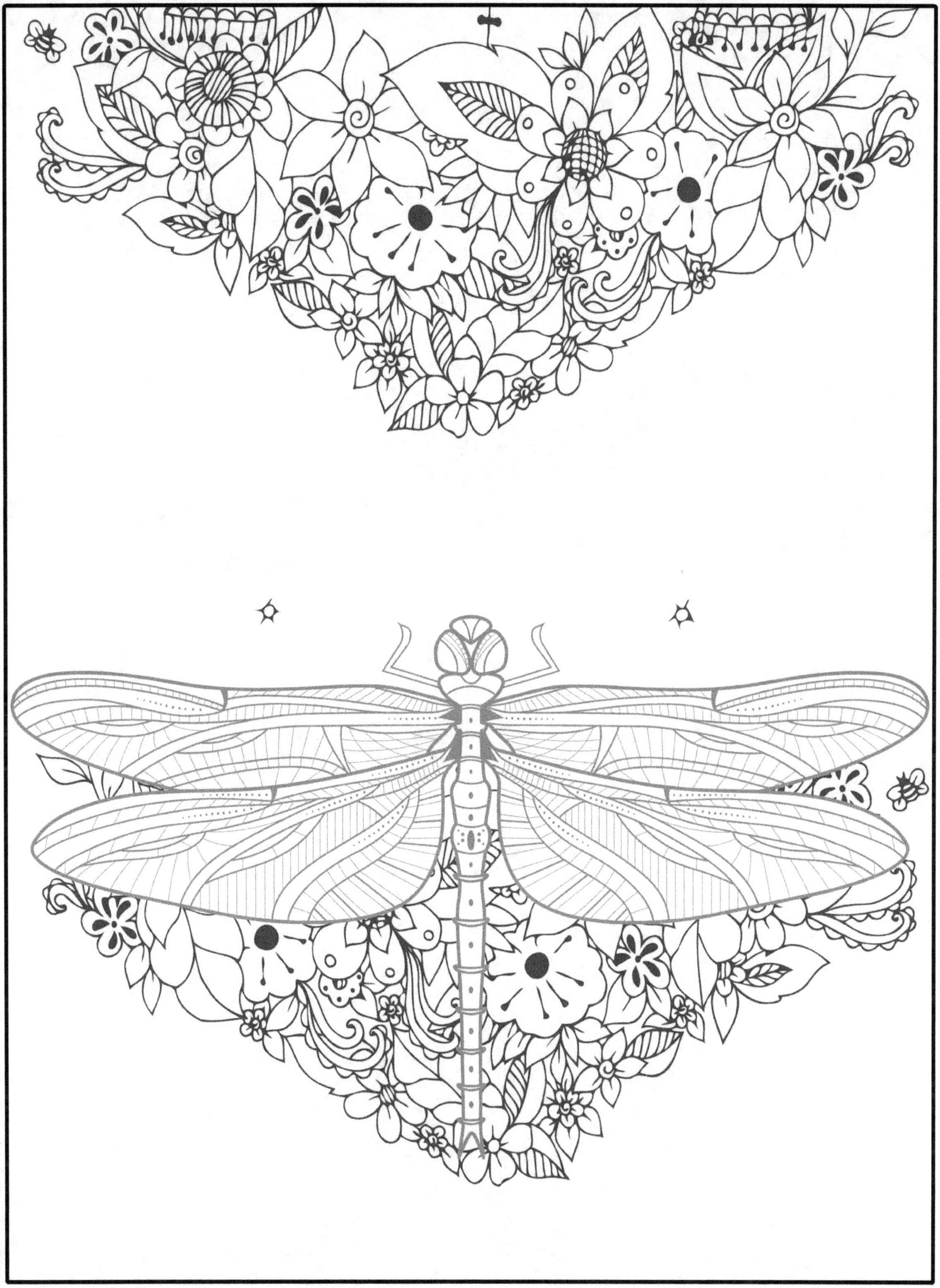

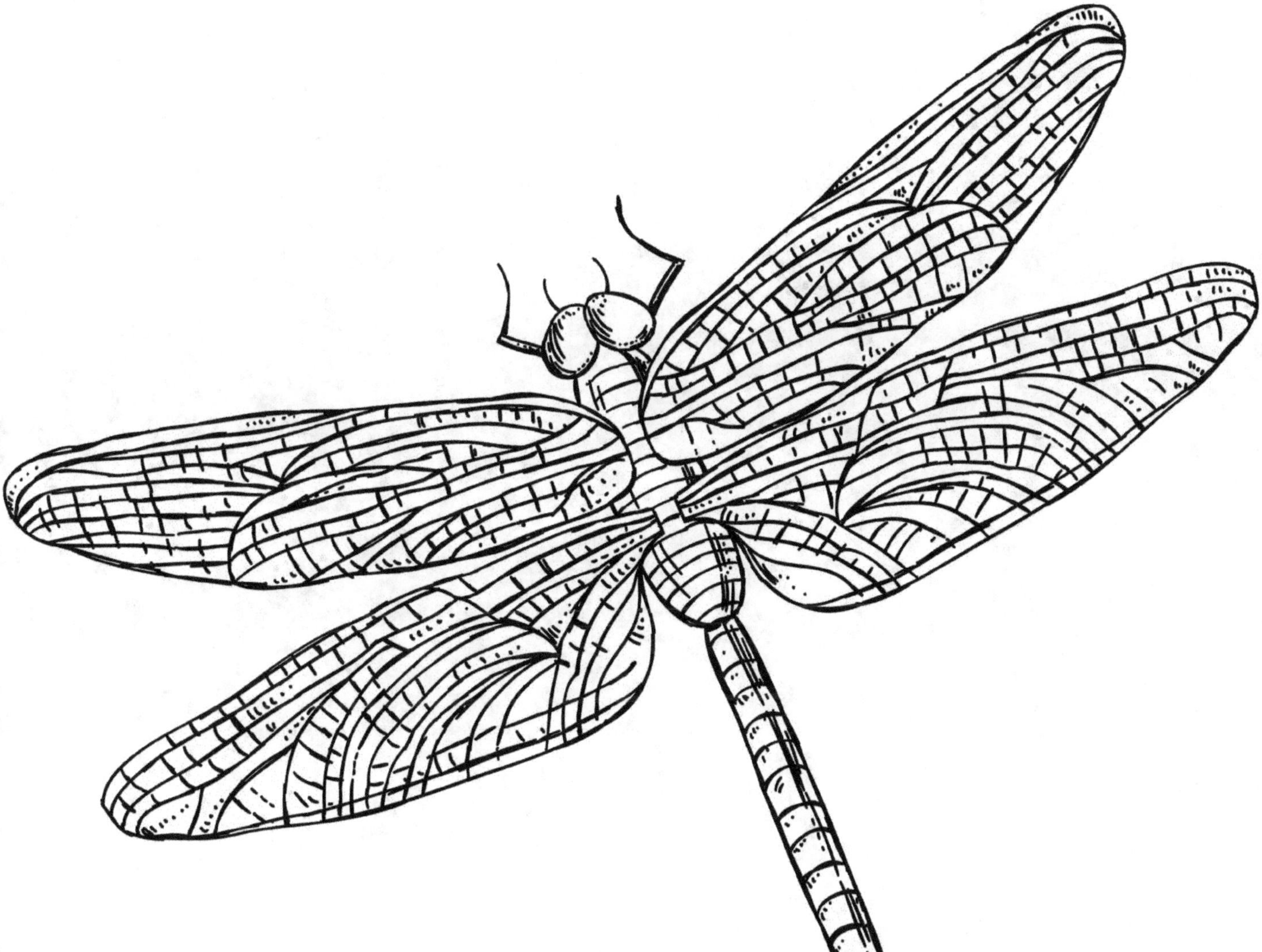

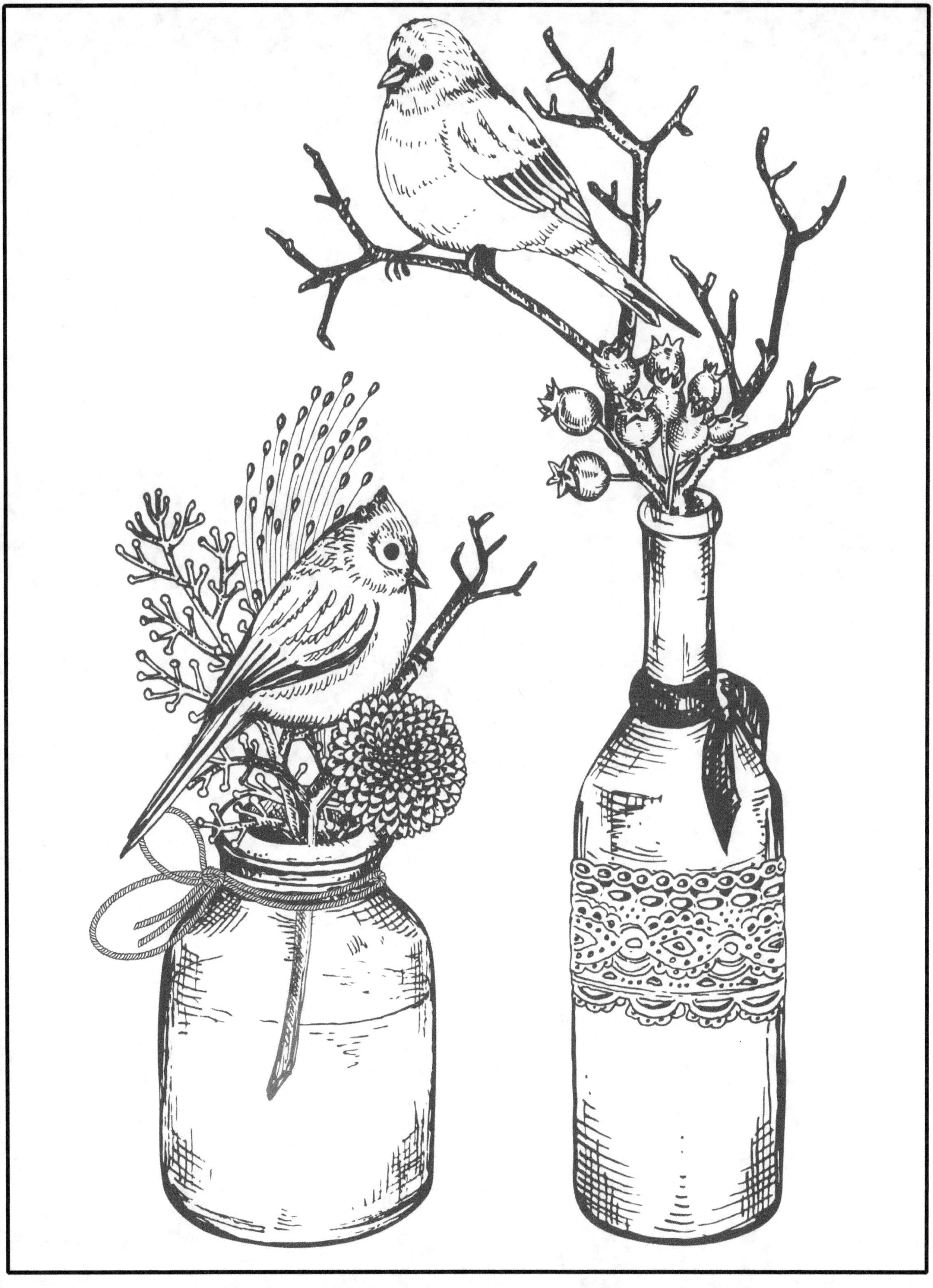

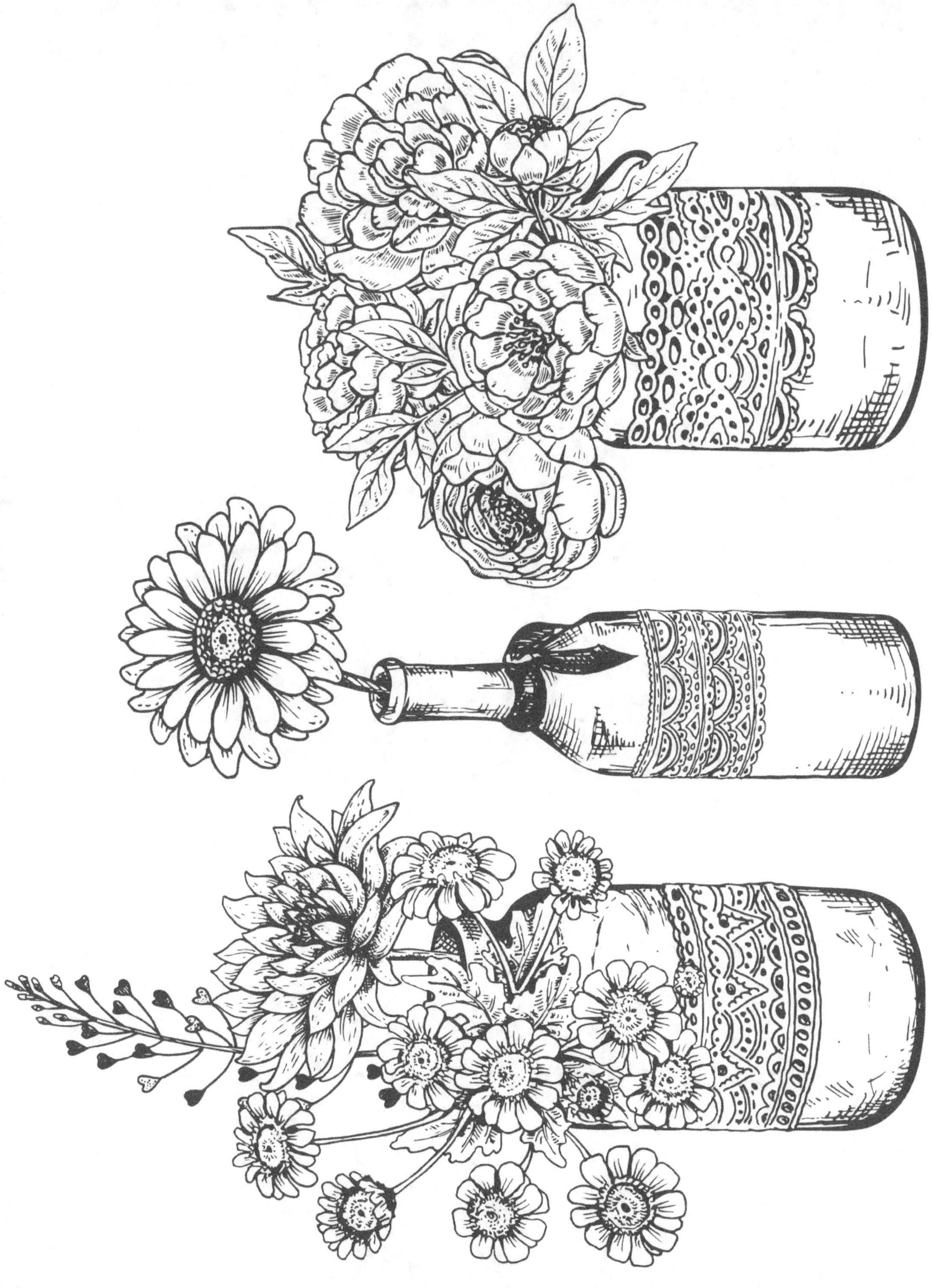

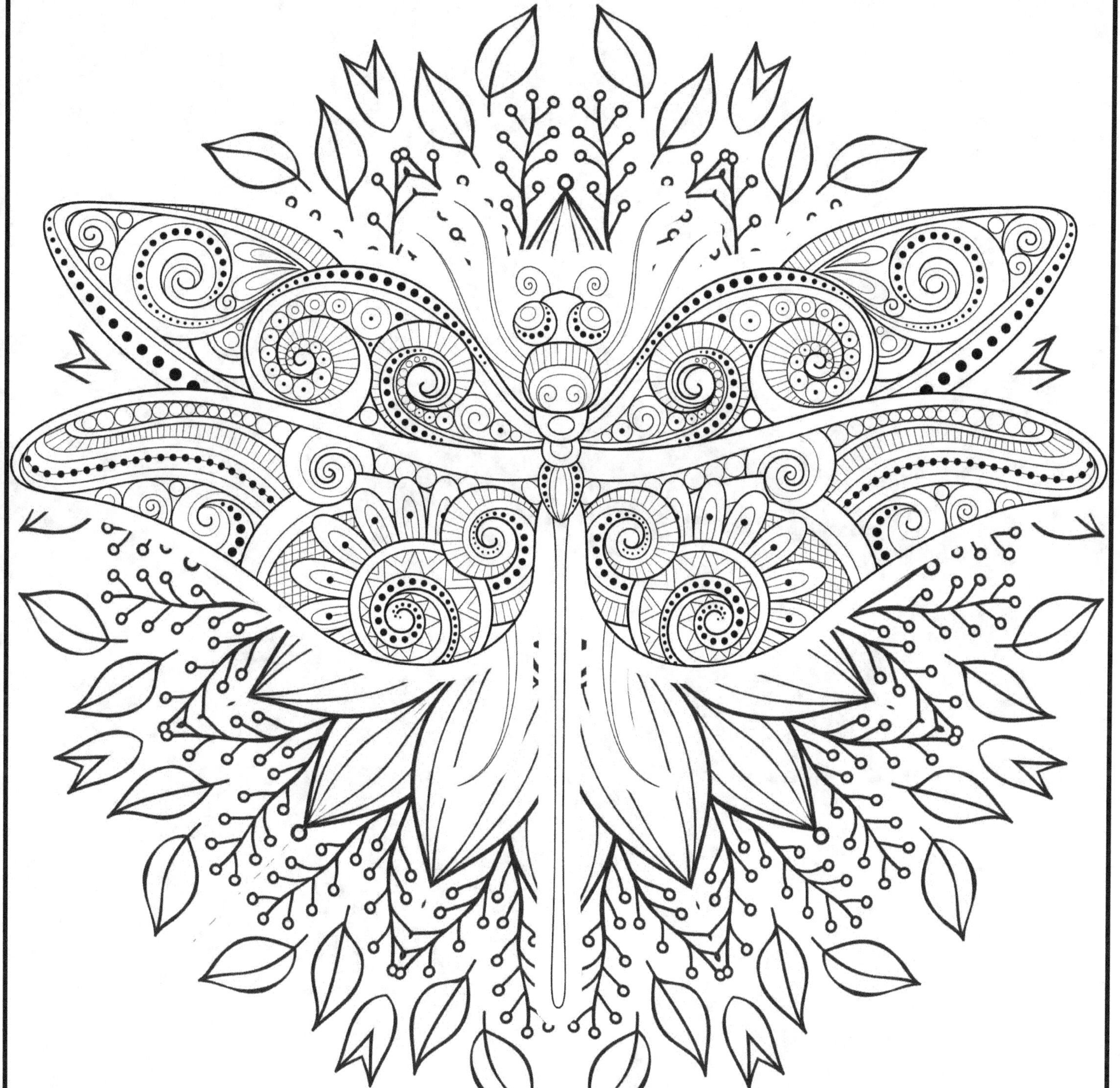

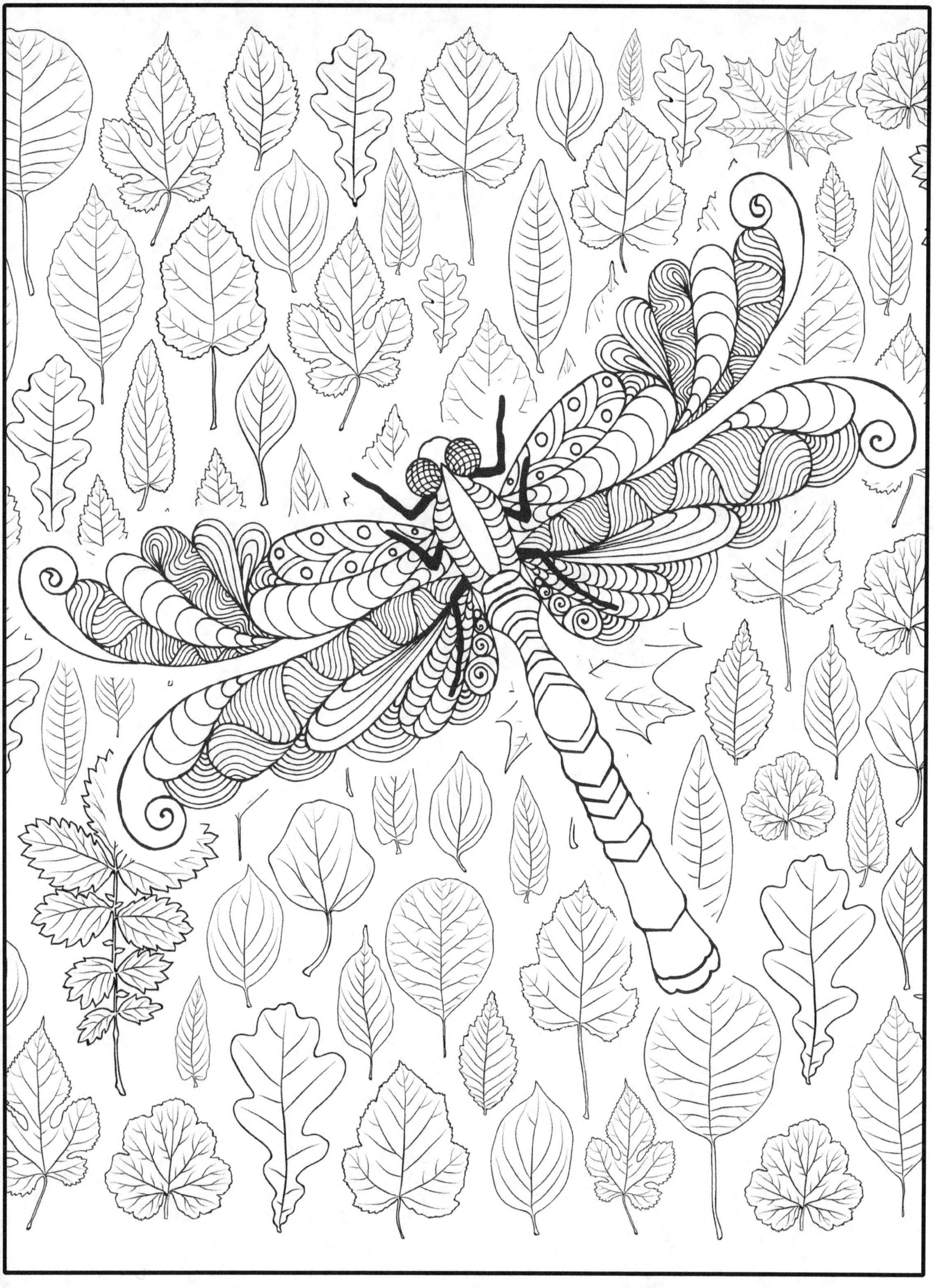

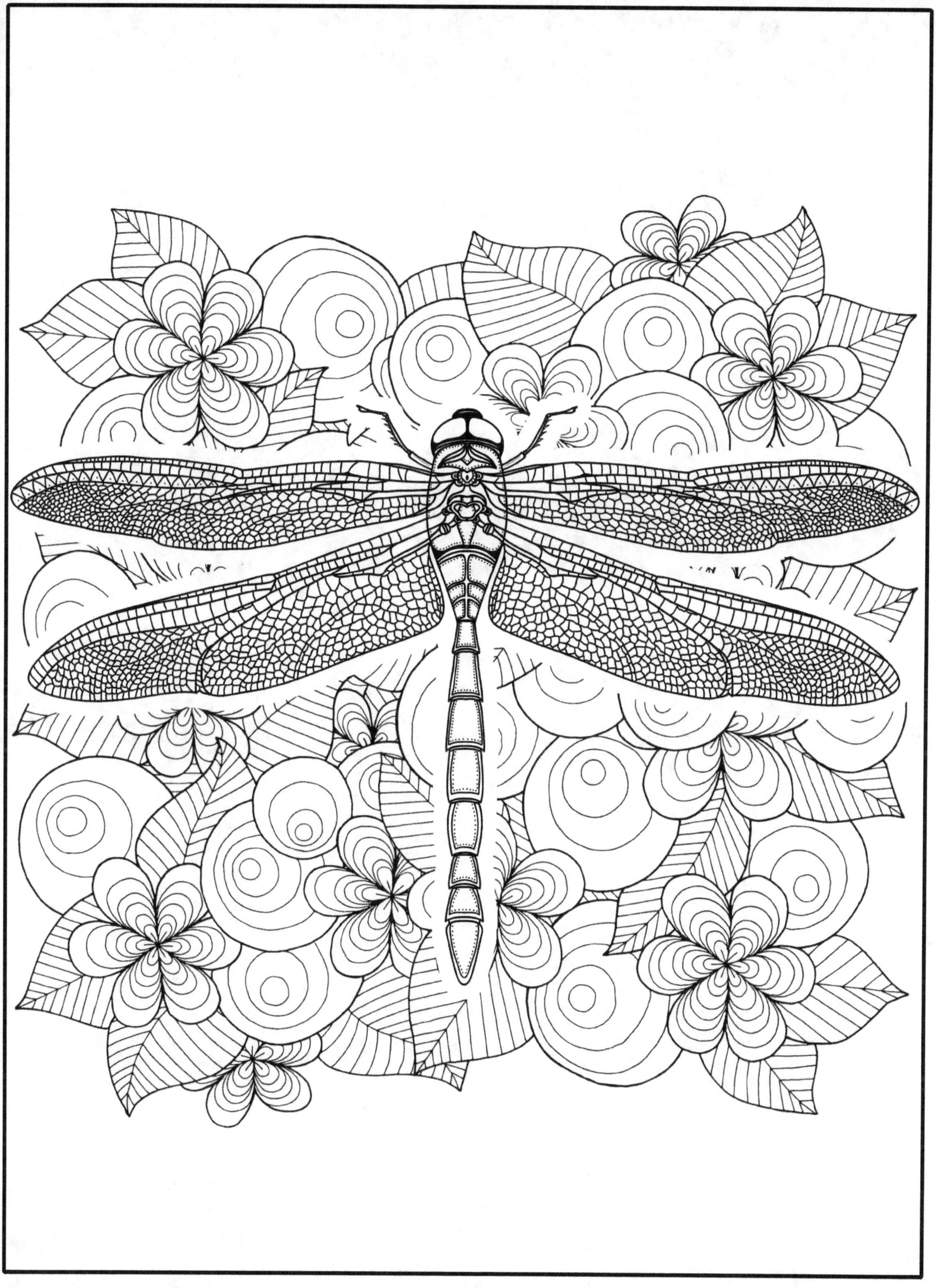

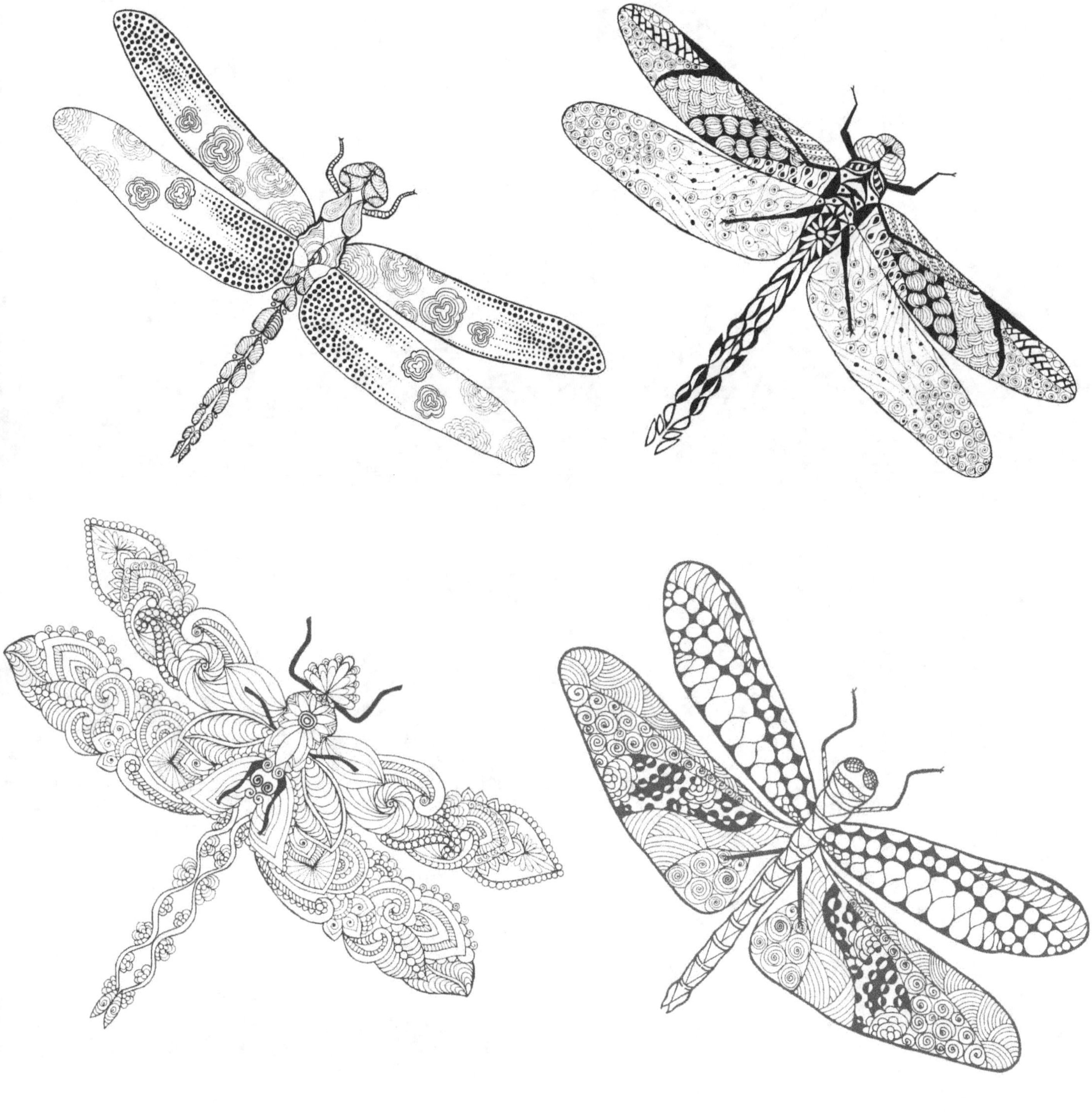

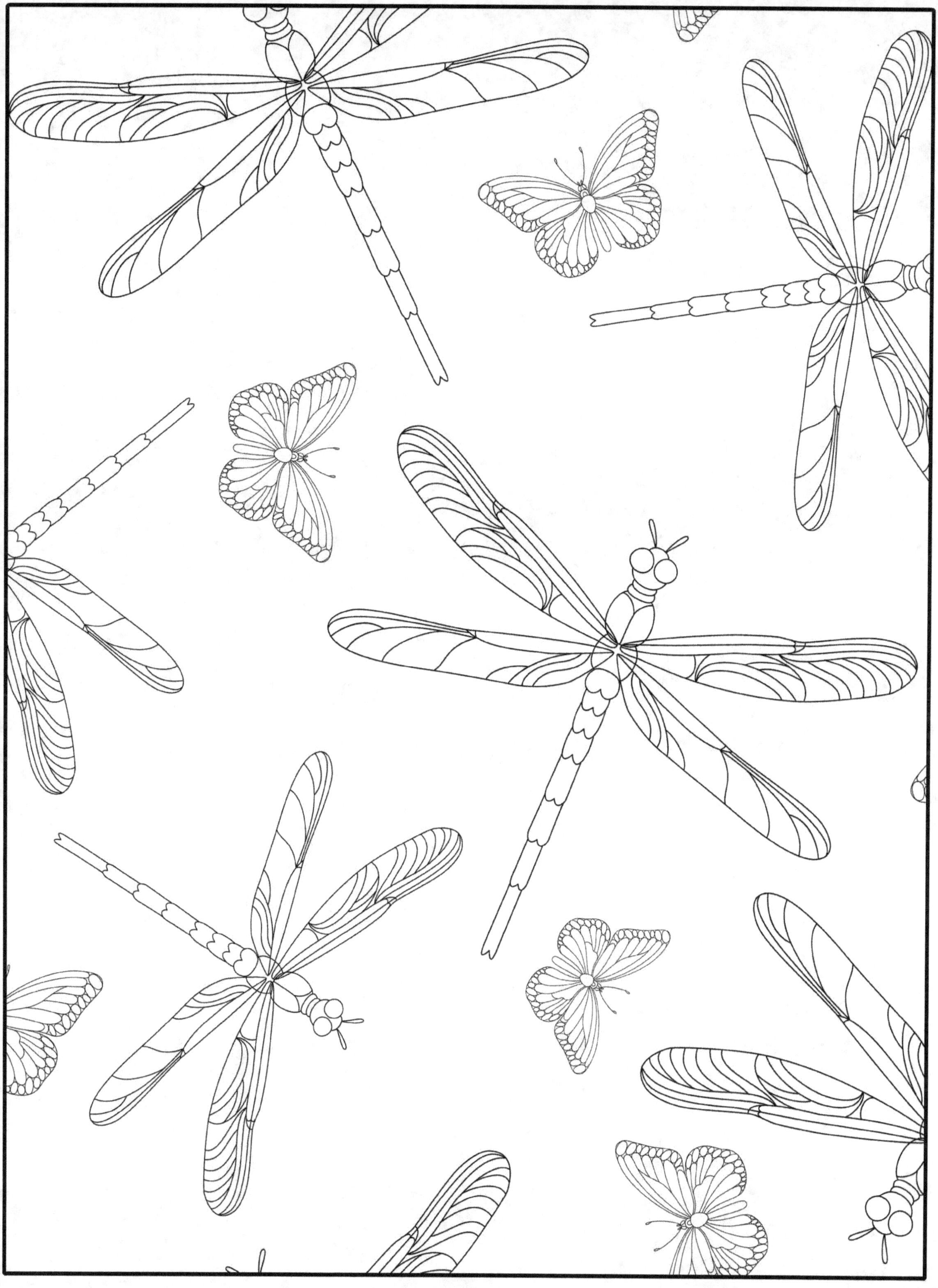

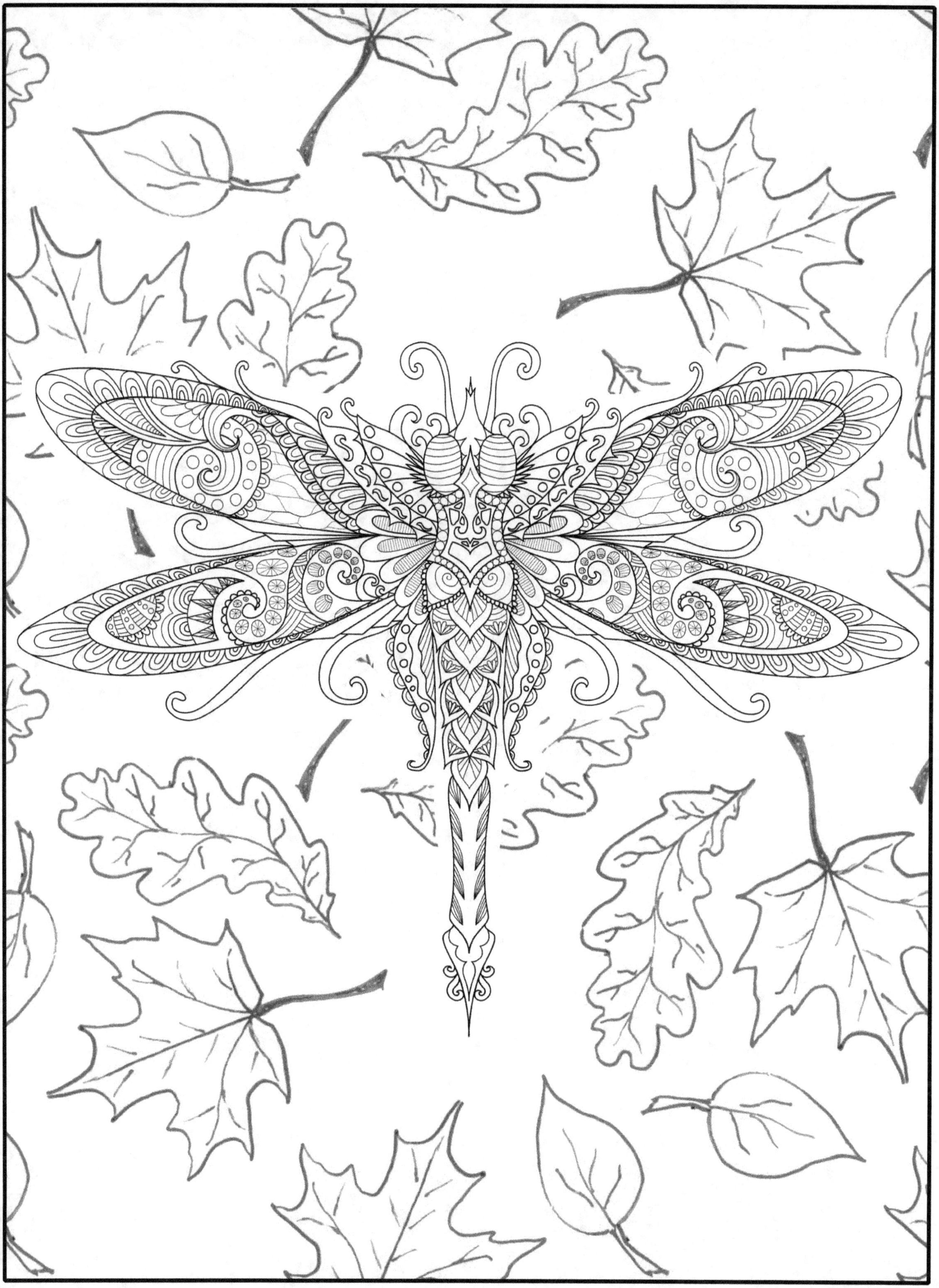

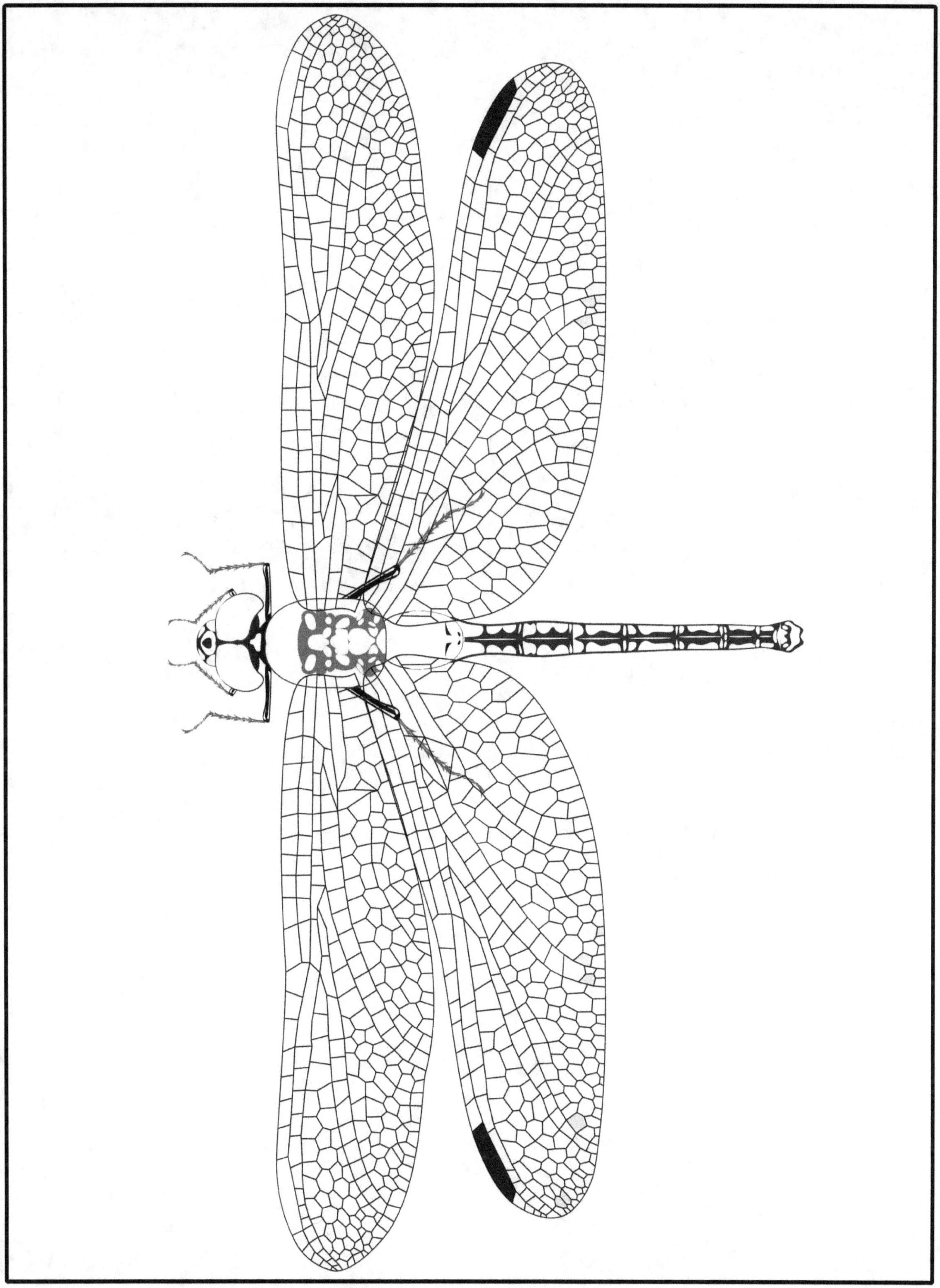

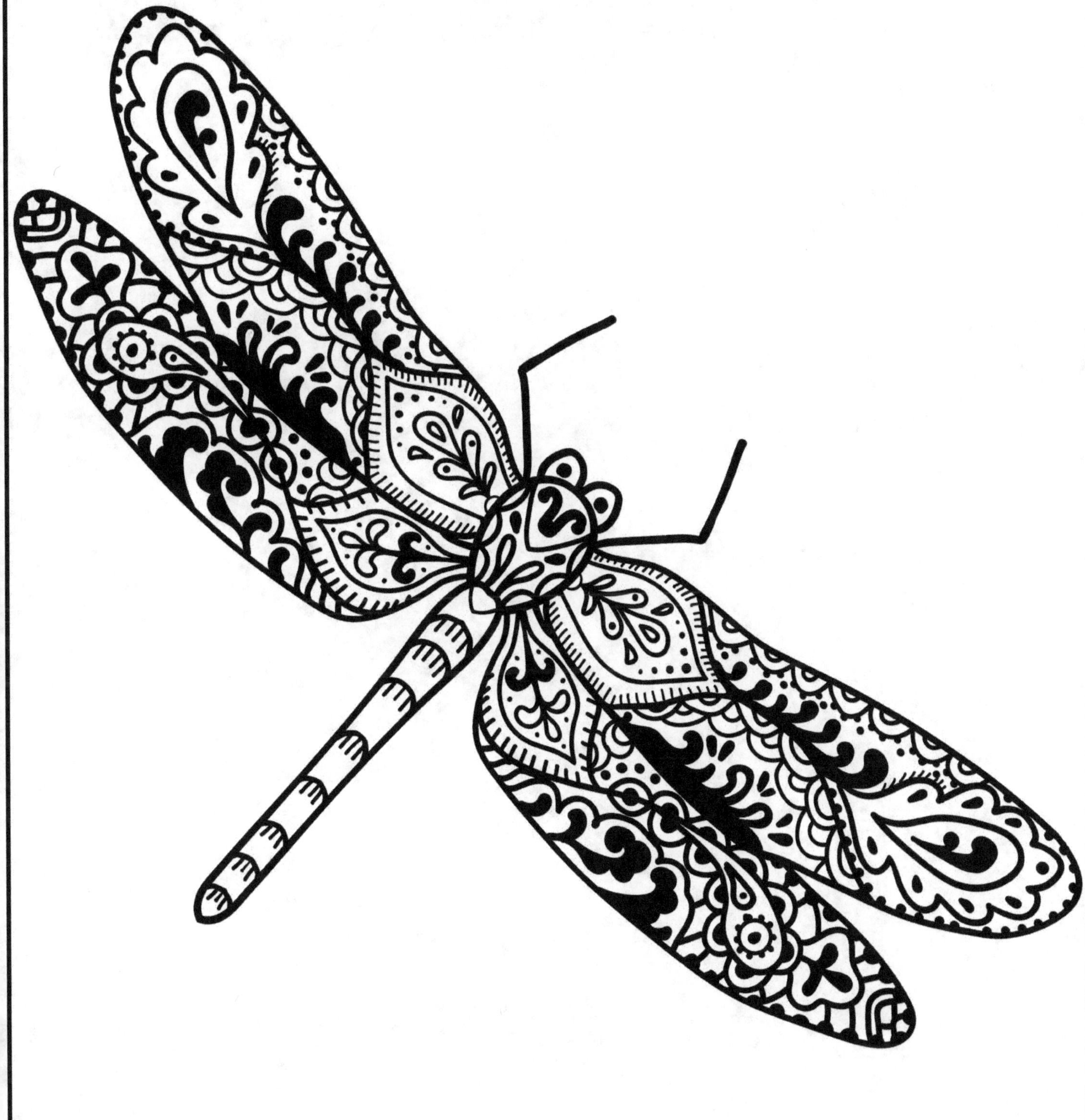

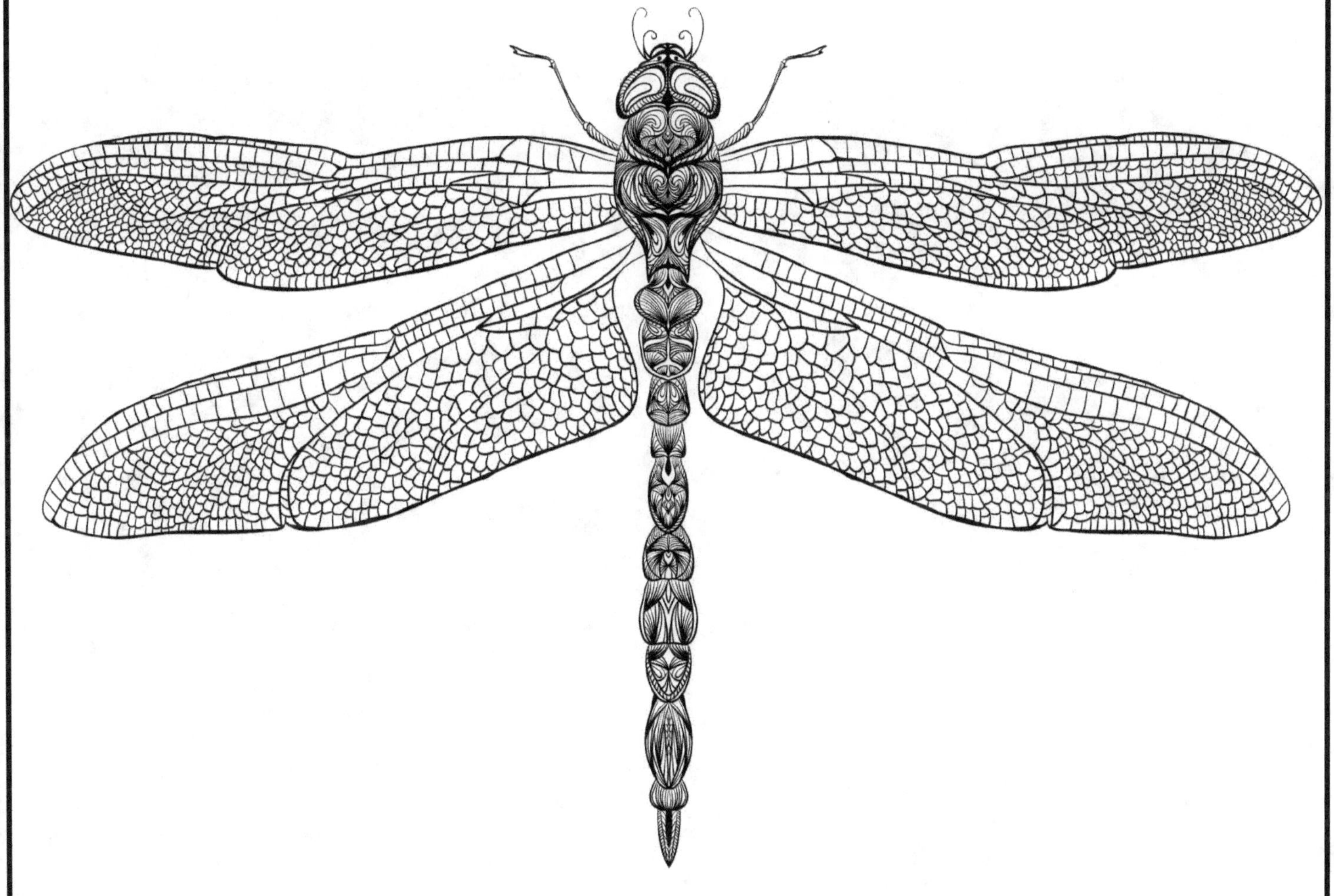

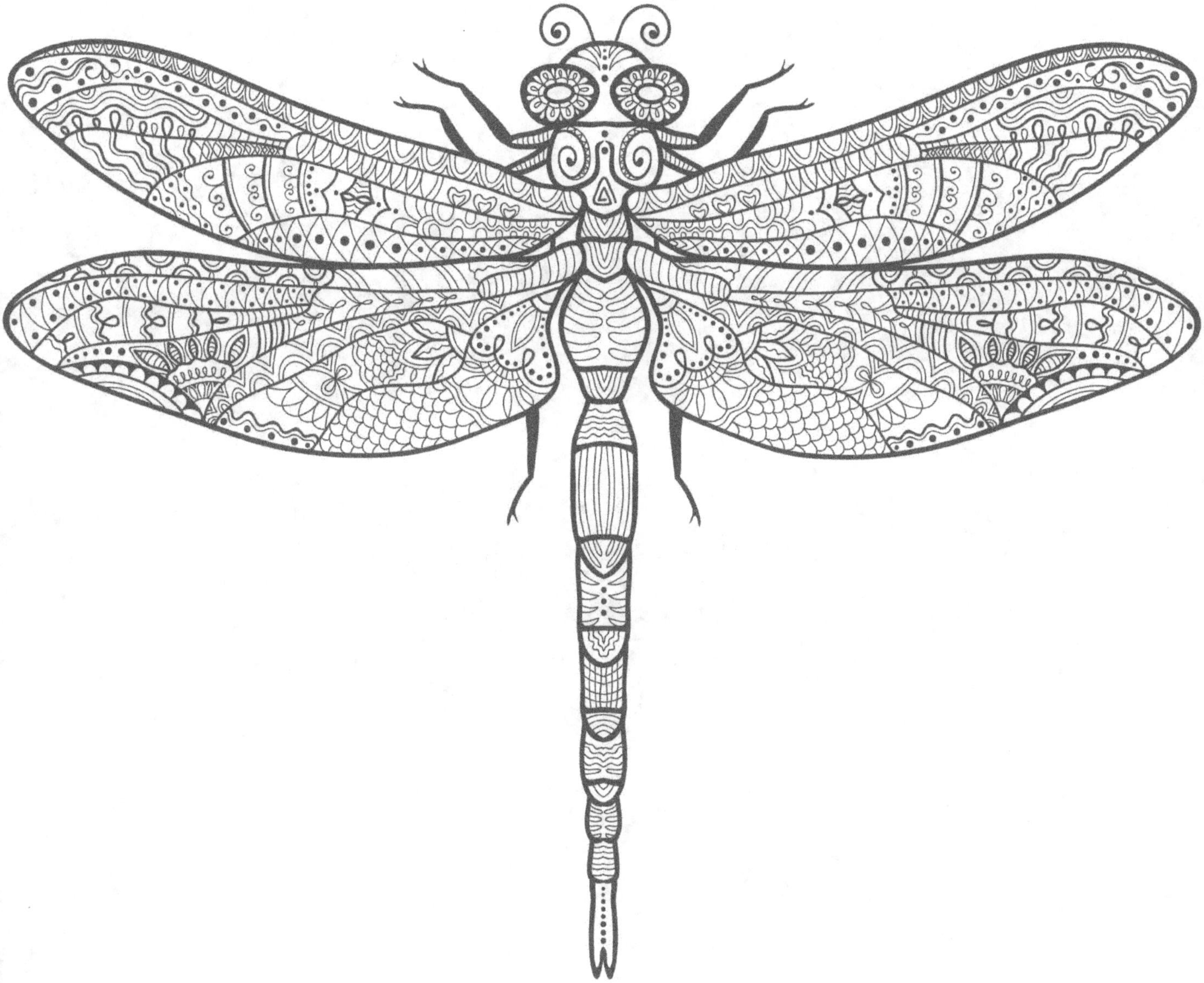

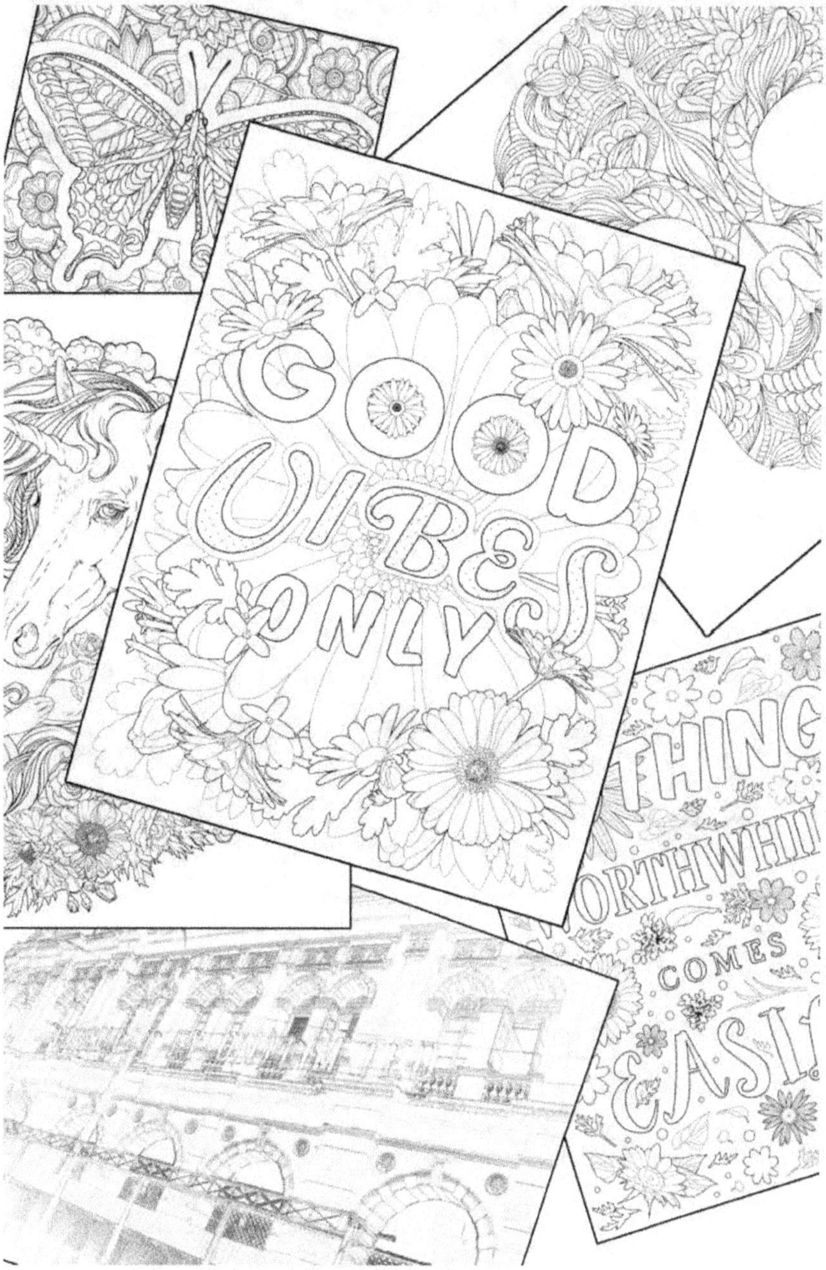
GOOD
VIBES
ONLY
THING
WORTHWHIL
COMES
EASI

www.ingramcontent.com/pod-product-compliance
Lightning Source LLC
Chambersburg PA
CBHW081123180526
45170CB00008B/2974
* 9 7 8 1 5 4 5 2 8 8 4 9 8 *